"As a former student of Mr. Strauss, I can attest to his profound impact on those fortunate enough to cross his path. His classroom was more than a place to learn; it was a space to grow, laugh, and be seen. *A Lasting Impact in the Classroom and Beyond* captures the heart of the educator I remember—unwavering in his belief in students, honest in his humor, and generous in sharing his wisdom. This book is a gift to anyone in education or considering the journey. Strauss didn't just teach English; he taught life, and these pages reflect the legacy of a teacher who truly cared."
Emerald Woodland, *Arizona State University Professor of Educational Leadership*

"*A Lasting Impact in the Classroom and Beyond* is a must-read for anyone considering a career in education. This book offers the optimism, joy, and love that can make teaching sustainable, and the wisdom of life lessons to help teachers become positive catalysts in the lives of young people. It is essential reading for anyone looking to gain deeper insight about educating the next generation."
Dr. Patrick Jones, *Senior VP, The Mind Trust; Former Strauss Student*

"Larry Strauss helped me immensely through my first few years teaching, and now speaks to a generation of other teachers trying to grasp the realities of classrooms in the post-COVID-19 era. He masterfully captures what makes education an arduous yet ultimately rewarding endeavor. This book offers an honest and authentic account of what it means to be an educator and will be the reason why someone becomes or remains a teacher, a role that is more necessary now than ever."
Elias Gonzalez, *L.A. Public School Teacher of Ten Years*

A Lasting Impact in the Classroom and Beyond

Are you sick of classroom management advice that doesn't match your daily existence or address the realities of the classroom? In this helpful new book, renowned educator Larry Strauss provides an honest examination of the challenges we face as high school teachers, not the least of which are the minds and temperaments of teenagers, the kind of empathy that can meet the most daunting teaching conditions, and the commitment required of us to succeed—but also the profound rewards of achieving that success.

Strauss provides meaningful ways for teachers to forge their path to success and have a lasting impact on students. Topics include getting to know and love your kids, even—or especially—in their worst moments; practicing intentional fairness and committing to relentless empathy; understanding who teenagers are; focusing on progress; setting modest goals and a vision of the long term; creating authenticity; encouraging kids to speak up; and making differentiation manageable. He also shows you how to stay committed and prioritize your sanity at the same time by overcoming compassion fatigue, getting support, protecting your time, and keeping your sense of humor.

The book offers hope to educators who feel themselves veering toward surrender but are still looking for a path to ultimate success. With honesty, insights, inspiration, and humorous examples, you'll have a blueprint for a successful and rewarding career in the classroom.

Larry Strauss has taught thousands of children in South Los Angeles since the early 1990s and has mentored dozens of new and struggling teachers since the early 2000s. A National Board Certified teacher since 2003, he created an AP program and an athletic program at his school and saw both programs blossom—and coached an LA City basketball championship team whose coaching staff included the captain of the school's very first basketball team 23 years earlier. In his youth, he was a New York subway graffiti writer, a stand-up comic, a disco bouncer, and, for two seasons, a writer on the first-generation Transformers cartoon. Bluesky Handle: @Lstrauss

Also Available from Routledge
Eye on Education
www.routledge.com/k-12

What Great Teachers Do Differently, 3rd Edition: 19 Things That Matter Most
Todd Whitaker

Your First Year, 2nd Edition: How to Survive and Thrive as a New Teacher
Todd Whitaker

The Heart-Centered Teacher: Restoring Hope, Joy, and Possibility in Uncertain Times
Regie Routman

Passionate Learners, 3rd Edition: How to Engage and Empower Your Students
Pernille Ripp

Dear Teacher: 100 Days of Inspirational Quotes and Anecdotes
Brad Johnson

Becoming a More Assertive Teacher: Maximizing Strengths, Establishing Boundaries, and Amplifying Your Voice
Brad Johnson and Jeremy Johnson

A Lasting Impact in the Classroom and Beyond

Knowledge and Insight for Brave Teachers

Larry Strauss

Routledge
Taylor & Francis Group
NEW YORK AND LONDON

Designed cover image: © Getty Images

First published 2025
by Routledge
605 Third Avenue, New York, NY 10158

and by Routledge
4 Park Square, Milton Park, Abingdon, Oxon, OX14 4RN

Routledge is an imprint of the Taylor & Francis Group, an informa business

© 2025 Larry Strauss

The right of Larry Strauss to be identified as author of this work has been asserted in accordance with sections 77 and 78 of the Copyright, Designs and Patents Act 1988.

All rights reserved. No part of this book may be reprinted or reproduced or utilised in any form or by any electronic, mechanical, or other means, now known or hereafter invented, including photocopying and recording, or in any information storage or retrieval system, without permission in writing from the publishers.

Trademark notice: Product or corporate names may be trademarks or registered trademarks, and are used only for identification and explanation without intent to infringe.

ISBN: 978-1-032-88659-6 (hbk)
ISBN: 978-1-032-88352-6 (pbk)
ISBN: 978-1-003-53893-6 (ebk)

DOI: 10.4324/9781003538936

Typeset in Palatino
by KnowledgeWorks Global Ltd.

Dedication

For Louisa and Amalia—the future is bright with you in it

Contents

Meet the Author xiv
Preface. xvi
Appreciations xx

Introduction: Who Am I to Tell You About
Being a Teacher 1

Part I: You're as Ready as Anyone Has
Ever Been: All You Need Is an Open Mind
and an Open Heart 7

  1 Why Bother 9

  2 Shuck the False Notions 15

  3 Teenagers Are Teenagers. 20

Part II: Getting Your Groove: Effective Teaching Is
Affective Teaching 25

  4 Develop Your Brand. 27

  5 You've Kind of Got to Love Kids. 35

  6 And Get to Know Your Students. 41

  7 It's All About Them Always. 50

  8 Be a Presence in Their Lives. 60

9 Some Focus on Fairness.........................67

10 Empowerment Is Power 75

**Part III: Win Win: Success Is the Means
and the Ends....................................83**

11 Modest Goals and a Vision of the Long Term 85

12 Bring the Passion 90

13 Nice Is Not Weak 93

14 Fun Is the Goal, Always 99

15 Plan to Be Spontaneous......................106

16 Create Authenticity 111

17 Manageable Differentiation..................116

18 Success Is the Means and the End............123

19 Noise.......................................129

20 What They Call Classroom Management 136

21 We Are All Beginners 148

**Part IV: All in for the Kids and Ourselves:
Keeping the Fire without Being Consumed 151**

22 Dispatching Demands and Weathering Fads 153

23 Try to Be an Ally with Admins 162

24 Try Being a Partner with Parents............170

25 Protecting Kids from Travesty of Test Mania 178

26 Don't EVER Lose Your Sense of Humor 184

27 Change Is the Constant 194

28 Teaching through the Learning Tools of Evasion
    and Distraction 202

29 Sanity First, Martyrdom Is Overrated 208

30 Don't Let Heartbreak Bury You 213

31 Give and Get Support 219

32 Keep Pushing for Systemic Change 224

Meet the Author

Since the early 1990s, Larry Strauss has taught thousands of high school students and mentored dozens of teachers in South Los Angeles. Central to his work is the belief that all children want to learn and succeed and that all teachers who understand and appreciate this and who love their students can have a meaningful and lasting impact on them.

His experience as a writer and storyteller has informed his teaching and mentoring practice: we are trying to help kids begin the story of their precious lives while we construct the narratives of our teaching careers; reaching kids and inventing ourselves as teachers requires deep insight into character, setting, story, and backstory. Strauss is particularly proud of the dozens of students who have gone on to become educators, many of them in the same community.

A National Board Certified teacher since 2003, Strauss created and helped build an AP program and an athletic program at his school. He coached the basketball team to a Los Angeles City basketball championship with a coaching staff that included the captain of their very first basketball team 23 years prior. In 2018, he was honored by the city, school district, and the Los Angeles Rams football team for his years of service and dedication to helping young people in and out of the classroom.

Strauss is the author of five novels and numerous non-fiction titles, including *Students First and Other Lies*, a collection of essays mostly about education. Since 2019, he has been an opinion columnist for *USA Today*. Other op-eds and other non-fiction have appeared in *The Guardian*, *The Bulwark*, *The Huffington Post*, and *Ambassador*, an inflight magazine of the now defunct Trans World Airlines. Some of his columns and stories have been excerpted in college textbooks and anthologized in collections.

In his youth, he was a New York subway graffiti writer, a stand-up comic, a discotheque bouncer, and, for two seasons, a writer on the first-generation *Transformers* cartoon—all experiences that have, in various ways, informed his teaching practice and his approach to helping new and struggling teachers. Bluesky handle: @LStrauss

Larry Strauss on a beach field trip with his students

Preface

On a JFK to LAX flight one evening in the early 2000s, I was hunched over a mountain of student papers teetering on my tray table, furiously marking and grading, when a man across the aisle asked me the obvious—was I a teacher—then sheepishly said, "I guess I didn't have to ask."

We struck up a conversation as people used to do on airplanes before there were entertainment centers on the backs of seats and on our portable electronic devices. He was a screenwriter with a few credits and a lot of things in the works. He got me talking about my life as a high school teacher in South Los Angeles—the challenges, the absurdities, and the many joys. I thought he was picking my brains for his possible next spec script, but by the end of the flight, he'd taken my phone number and email in the hope of arranging to visit my school and meet with my principal on the off chance she might hire him on an emergency credential for one of our school's unfilled positions.

A few months later, we were working together.

I wasn't thinking about recruiting a teacher that evening—just trying to chip away at that mountain of papers, but somehow, according to what my fellow passenger told me years later, I managed to convey something resembling passion and purpose, and somehow I persuaded him to go home and reconsider his life. In that sense, perhaps, all educators are potential recruiters working on behalf of kids to mitigate the persistent dearth of teachers.

I have mixed feelings about that. The people who run school systems and the parents and politicians who oversee them need to eliminate the teacher shortage by making the job of teaching more sustainable, and it probably doesn't help our cause to convince anyone to take the job as is, but the kids in our schools cannot wait for systemic change, and perhaps the battle is best fought from within. I'd like to think that everyone I have influenced to become an educator—mostly former students of mine—is down for the students and ready to push for systemic change.

That is the kind of influence I hope this book will have.

Helping new and struggling teachers is, like teaching itself, a test of imagination.

Imagining our most challenged and challenging students overcoming their fear and insecurity and hostility and distraction, even for a few moments, keeps us—and them—going until that moment of discovery or self-discovery, the epiphany or just a spasm of maturity that lets us and them know they can learn and succeed.

It is the same for those of us working with new and struggling teachers. We have to imagine their success so they can imagine it and believe in the possibility while they work toward it.

I always try to be realistic with the teachers I help—realistic about our job, the awesome responsibility of it, and what it can take to thrive in it. I have tried to structure this book in a way that conveys that same realism—to go along with the idealism I hope you possess and are able to nurture.

Whatever has brought you to teaching, we can never have enough good reasons to be there with the kids and that is a great place to begin. So is challenging all the mythologies about teaching and about teenagers. It all starts with who we are and who we will be as teachers—and loving and understanding the kids we teach. Teaching is personal, and relationships are how kids become reachable and teachable. Appealing to their sense of justice and fairness is essential, and that is best accomplished when we locate our own power by empowering our students.

Perspective and patience—with our students and ourselves—are essential, and so is a willingness to carry the enthusiasm for kids until they feel it. Kindness goes a very long way and is more powerful than many of us might imagine. One of the best expressions of kindness is our sensitivity to student boredom and our understanding that the best cure is to make at least some aspect of the learning fun. Spontaneity and authenticity are among the most effective tools to that end and are the essence of our mission—bringing the curriculum to life for all our students.

That, in turn, is the first big step toward managing the sometimes radically disparate abilities, sensibilities, and interests of the kids in our classes to ensure that they all have access to success. In fact, success is as much a tool for us as it is a goal for us and our students. To accomplish it, we need to be able to differentiate constructive from destructive student noise and get beyond the concept of "managing" student behavior—though we may, at times, need to manage it. All of this is a continual process, one I remain engaged in even as I write this. Probably the greatest challenge for me writing this book is that I am still teaching and so still learning things, sometimes constantly. There are plateaus to this work, but the summit will always remain elusive.

It can be, however, a beautiful and life-affirming process—if we are prepared to navigate and in some cases protect ourselves from all the influences and potential toxins coming from outside the classroom. That means prioritizing students and student learning over administrative folly, including over-testing, but also getting along with admins as well as parents, and constructing ourselves a viable and reliable support system so we can keep our sanity, laugh a little—or a lot—and protect our time, our mental health, and our emotional well-being. It means being ready to roll with the punches of change, technological and otherwise, and, as much as anything, it means continuing to push for positive change in our schools and the education system while we do the best we can for our students with what we have.

Because I teach in Los Angeles, and because most of the teachers I now mentor do not work at my school, we do most of our work—the venting and encouraging, crying and consoling, ranting and laughing, and strategizing—on our phones while we are traversing the clogged streets and freeways in various parts of the city. And yet we often feel more connected in this way, perhaps because our disembodied voices require us to engage our imaginations to attach a person to a voice, and perhaps, at the same time, there is clarity and power in a voice filling the inside of our car as we stare at the sea of red tail lights before us and that makes it easier to recall the words of encouragement and solace and the advice in a moment of classroom crisis and despair.

I hope the words in these pages can have the same kind of effect—though please don't attempt to read them while driving (how's that for a cheap plug of the audiobook?)

These car conversations also provide a clarity, a purity about those special moments when a mentee no longer needs to be mentored and we are just colleagues talking about our day in the classroom, commiserating and congratulating and conspiring. It is those moments that give me the audacity to believe that my experience, my own trial and error—which are still occurring every teaching day of my life—can help brave teachers I've never even met (not even on a phone or in a car in traffic) find themselves as inspired and inspiring educators.

Appreciations

First and foremost, thanks to my wife and fellow educator, Eleanor, whose heart and mind are my greatest inspiration and resource. And to my daughter and fellow educator, Carly, whose talent and passion for art and for teaching art are my other greatest inspirations.

And to my other children, Sean and Nora, whose courage and dedication to excellence inspire me every day and who, along with Carly, have given me more love and understanding than any parent can hope for.

I've got to give a big shout-out to my granddaughters; their passion for learning, discovery, self-expression, and self-exploration are humbling reminders of the awesome responsibility and privilege of being a teacher—and a grandfather.

Special thanks to Lauren Davis, a wonderful editor who has believed in this book from its inception, recognizing the value of classroom experience and the importance of sharing it on a large scale with brave new teachers.

Now comes the hard part—how to thank all the colleagues and students who helped me become a teacher. Thanks to all the teachers I have had the privilege to work with over the years, especially those who first welcomed me as a colleague and partner—Kevin Kennedy, Myra Boime, Roger Butcher, Sherwin Boucher, Moses Robinson, and Rob Hart—and those with whom I shared laughter as well as outrage, enough to endure the most challenging moments—Ted Hajjar, Lance Wylie, Sean McCue, Honest Chung, James Coffield, Michael Ulmer, Irena Kornilova, Josh Krawitz, Andrew Wagner, and the late Charles Charlap.

And thanks to all the many other teachers who have helped and inspired me over the years and the many who have allowed me to try to help them, along with those new teachers who were made by the school district to listen to my advice for an hour or two a week and who expressed great appreciation for my efforts—whether sincere gratitude or politeness, I am sincerely grateful for the kind words.

And also thanks to Natalie Battersbee, who first hired me and thought I was great long before that made any sense, and to Pam Jackson, who kept up that hype and showed me what great school leadership looked like. I would also like to thank Betty Washington, Donald Moorer and Terrence Mudd for showing me how administrators and teachers really can be partners and for always appreciating what matters to kids.

Immense gratitude for all the other admins—well, almost all—that I have worked with.

And, of course, I want to express my endless appreciation for the thousands of students who have taught me and continue to teach me what matters and how to make a difference for them, including the many who are now my professional colleagues and those who are now the parents of my students. I won't name-check any of them. My student appreciation list would fill an entire book on its own and I'd end up leaving at least someone out, and how would I live with myself?

Introduction

Who Am I to Tell You About Being a Teacher

If you're reading this, you are probably at least considering this teaching thing. I appreciate that interest, however enthusiastic or tenuous. There don't seem to be enough of us at the moment or for the foreseeable future. Teaching high school has never been easy, and there is a reasonable argument to be made that it has never been more challenging than right now.

This shortage of teachers in many schools is no fluke. Teacher pay across the U.S. remains woefully insufficient, and even the slightest gains come grudgingly. Working conditions are often defined by inadequate resources and insufficient administrative support to help manage classes overcrowded with students, many with formidable needs, most with mobile phones and an addiction to them that is, at least in part, responsible for a teenage mental health crisis we are on the front lines of.

And yet, the potential rewards of a career in the classroom have never been greater.

It Is Good to Be Needed

Any doubt that kids need talented, knowledgeable, compassionate, and committed teachers were obliterated by the distance learning disaster of the Covid-19 pandemic. Technology isn't going to replace us. In fact, the proliferation of computing power has made us even more essential.

Does this mean we will finally be paid what we deserve? Probably not. Salaries are improving in some places, and with generally decent health coverage and solid pensions in many school districts—job benefits that are sadly becoming scarce for many other workers—a career as a teacher need not entirely be an exercise in self-sacrifice.

Most teachers enjoy a reasonable degree of job security and job satisfaction that increases with time. The work of educating young people is vital and the accomplishments, while often difficult to feel in the moment, can start to multiply with time and experience. When adults who were once your students stop by to say that you changed their lives—or *saved* their lives—the daily frustrations and futilities become trivial.

I wish I had known about that during my early struggles in the classroom.

My Unlikely Entry into the Teaching Ranks

How I came to believe I should be a classroom teacher is so inane that I never told anyone until I began to mentor struggling new colleagues and thought it might help them feel less embarrassed about their own misconceptions.

I was in my late 20s and still chasing literary dreams with a few credits and a lot of near misses. I got hired to ghostwrite a wellness book with a cardiologist and media doctor and ended up tutoring his son, who was struggling with sixth-grade science. I discovered that I had a talent for explaining things I barely understood and a deep well of patience from growing up as the younger brother of someone with severe autism and other cognitive challenges.

Soon, I was referred to other affluent families in the area and found myself booked solid Monday to Friday in mansions and high-rise condos overlooking the city, witnessing high-end family dysfunction and the despair of children raised by nannies in a vast emptiness.

I tried my best to help those kids learn to read and write better, calculate and master the material they were supposed to know, and have fun doing so, but I was often asked by the parents—and sometimes by the nannies—to help those kids scam their teachers, showing them shortcuts, showing them how to write by writing things for them. It was a good education for an aspiring educator—a taste of reality, an up-close glance at distracted kids struggling to keep up.

It wasn't until after a few years doing this that I got a notion of becoming a classroom teacher in a public school. I was at the Beverly Hills Library where I would sometimes meet a seventh-grade boy whose house was being remodeled. I was trying to help him study for a geography test, but he kept being distracted by some nearby teenagers who were socializing loudly over their chemistry textbooks. I went over and told them to be quiet. I employed the faux toughness I'd manufactured as a scared kid navigating New York City streets and subways of the 1970s, and it worked. I scared those teenagers and they shut up, and suddenly, crazily, I saw myself as a high school teacher. I'm not sure there has ever been a flimsier or more misguided rationale for a career, even a brief one I imagined, in education—attracted by the idea of power through intimidation.

Sure enough, the reality of that decision was sobering. Trying to teach an actual classroom of students was overwhelming and humbling—and often humiliating. After a few days, I wasn't sure I'd last a year—or even a semester. My first novel had been bought by a major studio, so I was pretty sure I'd have to leave the classroom soon anyway. I never imagined my teaching career would so profoundly outlast my delusions of literary grandeur.

But soon, I fell in love with the kids, and that, along with the patience my brother had taught me, were my greatest survival tools. Having been a reluctant learner and marginal K–12 student proved an asset in trying to help the most challenged students I was supposed to teach.

The indelible memory of all my anxieties and failures during those first months and years in the classroom has helped me be a sympathetic, empathetic, and pretty effective mentor to struggling, less-experienced teachers. I am continually reminding them that it can take some of us a while to get good at this teaching thing, and we are well-served to be patient with ourselves as we ought to be with our students and to remember that our teaching circumstances may be far from ideal—just as are the lives of our students—and that we and our students may be performing remarkably well under those conditions.

A lot of people with an interest in becoming educators are idealists by nature. That idealism serves our students well, but if we apply it too much to ourselves too soon, it can burn us out. Few among us can survive, believing we can do it all. We must be realistic, especially when we are new. Staying positive and not being discouraged might, for a while, be our most urgent goals. The kids need us to be comfortable and confident. They need us to have lives outside of work, to come to them refreshed and optimistic. If you are a glass-half-full person, it will be easier. If you are not, become one as fast as you can.

A Lasting Impact

Like many of my colleagues, I have tried to be an advocate for systemic change in education. There is so much potential stifled by dysfunction, mismanagement, hubris, and corruption. It is tragic that the victims of all the politics, the fear and loathing, the ambition, and the myopia are the most vulnerable children. For more than three decades, I have sounded off to anyone I could get to listen, even briefly, and for the last 15 years, I have been writing columns for whoever will provide me a platform to complain about what is wrong with the system and suggest what I believe will improve things. Some of my early columns were collected in a book called *Students First and Other Lies*.

Though many of my complaints have resonated with other educators as well as parents and others, I am unsure of what, if any, impact any of it has made. I have seen improvements. For example, there has been a pretty strong recognition that small schools are more likely to serve their students, especially those most challenged. Also an acknowledgment of the absolute need for so-called education leaders to collaborate with those of us who perform the actual work of teaching children. But the gains are often slow and not always sustained in meaningful ways, and as I approach the end of my career in teaching, I do so without much of an expectation that anything much is going to change in the radical ways I might have hoped.

One of the things that hasn't seemed to change at all is how poorly we prepare new teachers. I don't doubt that those who work in university departments of education are inspiring their student teachers. Perhaps there just is no way to really prepare anyone for the shock of being the teacher in a high school classroom—especially if that teacher's own high school experience occurred in a very different environment. But our K–12 system continues to insist on hurling new teachers into some of the deepest waters of challenging classrooms (there is an alternative, which I have devised and screamed about, but I do not anticipate seeing it implemented any time soon).

Perhaps the sink-or-swim approach was intended to repel those of us who lacked the talent and commitment our kids deserve, but in reality, we are losing far too many aspiring educators with the talent, the commitment, and even the love. Few of us are willing to—and none of us should be expected to—martyr ourselves. So, ultimately, who survives is often determined by the luck of the draw. I am one of the lucky ones. I got hired to teach in a school that was a good fit for me. A last-chance school for at-risk kids provided me with the space to find myself as a teacher and the opportunity to connect with kids who had mostly had such a hideous school experience that it was easy to be a really good teacher in their eyes.

I have been mentoring new teachers for more than 20 years, and it only recently hit me that this work—listening to, empathizing with, encouraging, advising, and collaborating with—has a far greater impact on the lives of kids than all my columns and other complaining and reimagining of the system. Not everyone will be lucky enough to get hired at just the right school for them. Most do not. Hopefully, this book will help you make a fit out of the teaching circumstances, whatever they are, in which you find yourself.

Until recently, I cultivated a fantasy that upon my retirement from teaching, I would be replaced by one of the dozens of former students turned educators. In my most grandiose moments, I imagined the entire English department at my school comprised of students who had, at least in part, been inspired to become English teachers after being subjected to one or more of my classes, but such legacies are beside the point.

Our work as teachers leaves behind a trail of mostly intangibles. Human development and learning are always at least partly a mystery, and often, our greatest triumphs are undetectable, at least in the moment, and at least partly the result of an act of faith—believing in the hidden power and talents of our students.

It is that same kind of faith that I hope this book will help new, ambitious, and struggling teachers develop in themselves. I believe deeply in anyone who believes in children and the importance of trying to educate them in whatever condition we find them.

This book, in its own way, is also an act of faith—my writing it and, more importantly, your willingness to read it and consider what I have to say. I greatly appreciate that.

Part I
You're as Ready as Anyone Has Ever Been
All You Need Is an Open Mind and an Open Heart

1

Why Bother

One of the few things I remember from the credentialing classes I took was a hypothesis about the passions of most aspiring educators. Elementary school teachers, we were told, become educators in order to work with kids. High school teachers are more likely to be motivated by their interest in the subject they teach. I think that I have remembered that claim so vividly because I've seen so much evidence to the contrary—lots of high school teachers who have only a modest interest in the math or history or English or whatever they are teaching and who care deeply about their students.

There are many reasons why people become teachers, and I'm not sure any are inherently good or bad reasons. I thought it would be fun to tell teenagers what to do, but it didn't take long for me to discover that it was far more enjoyable to see students learn how to become independent thinkers and learners—and then start telling me what to do.

Do It for You

What all teachers have in common—or ought to anyway—is the same self-interest as other workers. We may enjoy all the admiration and appreciation from people who believe we are modern-day saints (though it can get annoying after a while), but we aren't saints and certainly shouldn't try to be.

Even those of us willing to work the hardest and do the most for the kids we are asked to teach are self-interested people, as we should be, and almost certainly do what we do, in no small measure, for the feeling it gives us. Sacrifice is a beautiful thing, but except in extreme circumstances (soldiers in war, teachers during a school shooting) we ought never believe we are engaged in an entirely selfless enterprise. Those of us who do the most for kids usually get the most out of teaching. Not just the appreciation of students and parents but the intrinsic satisfaction.

When I stay at work till 6:00 or 7:00 pm to help students write their personal statements for college—work that is an exhausting combination of writing instruction and psychotherapy—I drive home in a cloud of euphoria. I feel the same high after breaking up a fight or talking kids out of self-destruction or anytime my lesson hits just right and I can see the epiphanies lighting up the classroom. Even the small triumphs are, for me, a natural high.

These are the strongest reasons I can offer you for working at something that can take years of hard and sometimes frustrating work, making mostly incremental, often undetectable, progress.

Teaching is, for many reasons, important work. Really important work. Economic and social progress depend on our efforts. Democracy and our social fabric thrive on our success—and suffer from our failures. Great schools can be incubators for social justice and effective teachers can be one-person crime prevention programs. Becoming a secondary teacher and paying your dues to realize your potential is all but guaranteed to give you a vital role in the future of the human experiment…

The Practical Rewards (Such as They Are)

As I write this, teacher salaries vary pretty widely around the world with some Western European countries routinely paying six figures to secondary instructors and countries in other parts of the world less than $15K a year—though adjusting for the cost of living in these countries may substantially close this disparity. The same may be said for the U.S. where Massachusetts, New York, Connecticut, and California pay teachers an average salary of low to mid 90K while Florida, West Virginia, and other states pay an average teacher in the low 50K range—and every other state somewhere between these extremes.

Mostly these salaries are woefully inadequate for the work we do. They are an affront to us and, even more so, an affront to our students. That said, in my district (in California) a teacher with ten years' experience and National Board Certification can, teaching summer school and doing other paid extra work, make 150K to 160K a year.

So, yes, there are the summers off, unless you have a mortgage or would like to one day have one. Also, like cops and firefighters, most of us are eligible for a public pension, a pretty significant perk at a time when nearly half of all Americans are without sufficient potential retirement income.

Furthermore, for those not living in so-called "right to work" states, there is the possibility of job security. I have known teachers who, during budget shortfalls, have lost their positions, but those who wished to stay in teaching usually manage to land somewhere else. The mass teacher layoffs following the U.S. financial crisis of 2008 were profoundly disruptive and are a big part of why there is now a shortage of teachers to replace all the Boomer retirements, which is a reason anyone willing to take on the challenge of teaching has the job security of having few people available to replace them.

The Impractical and the Incalculable

A few years ago, I assigned a class of seniors, many of whom had after-school and weekend jobs, an article called "The Secret to Happiness at Work." In it, Harvard Business School Professor Arthur Brooks asserts that increases in salary only temporarily impact job satisfaction while the greatest factors in job satisfaction are what he calls "earned success" and "service to others."

By earned success, Brooks means a sense of accomplishment and confidence about one's ability. Most of my employed students agreed that how they felt about their job had a lot to do with how competent they felt doing it, and I couldn't help thinking that teaching is—though perhaps a little surprisingly—a perfect example.

Of course, many of us, myself included, spend our early years feeling a lot of futility and frustration. This probably explains, as much as anything, the attrition among teachers. But if we are able to survive the struggles, we can almost certainly enjoy many years of earned success. In fact, those early failures will boost those subsequent feelings of accomplishment. And there is never much doubt that we have earned that success through patience, endurance, hard work, and commitment. For many of us, the accomplishment carries into other areas of our lives.

> But if we are able to survive the struggles, we can almost certainly enjoy many years of earned success.

That teaching is an opportunity to gain satisfaction from being of service to others may seem obvious, though it actually isn't, at least not at first. Kids mostly feign indifference to us and can be quite convincing. I still have vivid memories of feeling I was having no impact on any of my students. I once felt so demoralized I retreated to my desk and put my feet up to let the kids know that if they didn't care—and to me, at that moment, those students didn't care at all—then neither did I. Almost immediately, two students approached me asking permission to see their counselor in order to change classes. They said they needed a teacher who would at least try. It was devastating and revelatory and, of course, I've never forgotten, and I have never since surrendered to anyone else's seeming apathy.

At the end of that term, the students gave me a card they'd all signed, many inscribing messages that seemed unreasonably nice given how things had gone that semester. Some of them mentioned things I had done or said that had made a difference to them. One said I was the first teacher who ever complimented her writing. Another recounted a story I'd told the class and said she would always remember it for inspiration.

It took a few years before I could fully understand how much I was helping students. Mostly in small ways. As the years pass, those accomplishments become more obvious. They accumulate and start to exponentiate. You see kids grow up. Some change the trajectory of their family history in profound ways. They graduate from college, become professionals, and raise children. They become productive people, good people.

I remember getting a visit from one such student who'd become a successful photographer, happily married, and I suddenly remembered his struggles and the fact that he had been born addicted to crack cocaine. I also remember the first time a kid in my class wrote about a middle school teacher who had changed her life—and I realized that inspiring teacher had been a student in my class.

Amid all of my ineptitudes as a first-year teacher and basketball coach, I somehow helped a young man through his extremely fraught adjustment to surviving outside the gang life. Every June after graduating, he sent me a Father's Day card and years later, now a middle-class father, he returned as an assistant coach, and I watched him help some of our student athletes survive their own crises and traumas.

By then, I'd seen dozens of former students become educators. Some attributed their decision to how much fun I and some of my colleagues seemed to be having. Other students have become journalists and writers. I am proud of those who've become social workers and tried to help the most vulnerable and troubled kids. I am equally proud of those who've advocated courageously for justice, including a Los Angeles County Sheriff who stood up for herself and other women being harassed on the job. I am proud, too, of all my former students who have served in the military, including a combat veteran now surviving the physical and emotional ordeal after tours of duty in Iraq and Afghanistan and proud of those who have courageously fought their own personal battles.

For many years now, I have found myself teaching the sons and daughters and nephews and nieces of many appreciative former students, and for many years I have heard my name called out by former students in supermarkets and shopping malls, the airport security lines and other public places and received countless messages of appreciation, often for moments of kindness and understanding I scarcely remember.

The appreciation is great, but I don't expect it. My satisfaction comes simply from knowing I've played some positive part in their lives.

Of course, the story of some former students isn't a happy one, and no teacher I know of is able to reach every kid every year. The heartbreak is real (and coping with it is the subject of a later chapter). Ultimately, I believe, there is still satisfaction in knowing we have tried and in staying committed always to doing better for all our students.

Sometimes our failures turn out not to be. One former student, who seemed unreachable and unteachable and was arrested and imprisoned before the end of his senior year, returned years later and told some of my colleagues and me that during his incarceration, he kept remembering all the things we'd told him for more than two years and that our words had saved him from despair and helped him rethink his life and commit to change.

I find that to be a wonderful image for any teacher at any stage of our career, especially when we are experiencing one of those moments when we are hearing our own inner voice asking if this is all really worth it.

2

Shuck the False Notions

It is nearly impossible to imagine what teaching is like until we are trying to do it, and even then, it takes time to gain perspective. Mostly, what we bring to our first day in the classroom are distorted impressions, vague memories from a K–12 student's perspective, and dramatic scenes dreamed up by screenwriters and performed by actors.

Though I never, as a child, imagined I would one day be a teacher, I watched *Room 222* and *The White Shadow* on television and saw a smart, understanding, and heroic teacher and a smart, courageous, and selfless coach, and the students and players who looked up to them and followed their guidance. Both are good examples to critique in this regard because they were quite well done and in many ways as realistic as the television medium allows.

What they don't show—because it wouldn't be good television drama or at all practical to show it—is the grind and the enormous burdens of being a full-time classroom teacher.

A Very Truncated Version of Teaching

I'll start with the coach on *White Shadow*. He is presumably also a teacher (in the first episode, his old friend the principal who hired him says that he will finally get to use his teaching certificate), but we hardly see him having to teach. All we see is Coach Reeves and his dozen or so basketball players and all the dramas on and off the court. He doesn't seem to have to deal with a full load of classes.

Unless you are a big-time high school coach hired by a well-financed private school, high school coaching isn't a full-time job and you are carrying five or six classes along with coaching responsibilities.

The same kind of misconception comes from *Room 222* in which Mr. Dixon is always seen teaching the same students. As with *White Shadow* and every other school-centered television show, the medium necessitates this fallacy. A show isn't going to write and cast the 150–250 students a real teacher is responsible for, so we don't see the immensity of the work, all those kids we have to teach, every day, and plan for, and intervene with. Even the task of learning all those names can be overwhelming! In my first year, I had a class with three boys named Jose Diaz, none of whom had a middle name, and two sets of identical twins. In another class was a Carlos Felix and a Felix Carlos and in another class Aishia, Iyesha, and Ayeesha, all pronounced the same. That spring, attendance at our school fell off drastically and each day a different 20 of 35 students would show up for class so that every lesson had to begin and end that day. How could a TV show or movie ever convey any of this? Why would they even want to?

Nor would we know this from having been a student or even from visiting and observing a class as we are told to or made to do as aspiring educators.

I recently rewatched some episodes of *Room 222* and was struck by its depiction of the exemplary teacher. He never stumbles, never forgets his train of thought or a student's name (though, again, he's only seemingly got one class). Still, there really are teachers like Mr. Dixon—I'd like to think that there is a little Mr. Dixon in my teaching—he makes it look so natural, so effortless, like John Keating in *Dead Poet's Society*. What we don't see are the years of hard work: planning, reflecting, stumbling, learning, and growing from all the failures. Inspired teaching is the product of that hard work and struggle. We don't see that on the screen.

Miracle Workers by Omission

We ought to have high hopes and expectations for ourselves, but it is as important to be patient and we need to be realistic, and movies can mislead us. The example that affected me most was *Stand and Deliver*, a film based on the true story of math teacher Jaime Escalante whose charismatic passion and commitment changed the course of history at Garfield High School in East Los Angeles.

Escalante really was that guy—and I heard it directly from some of his students when I was a substitute teacher at Garfield during his last year there. In the film about him, Escalante (played by Edward James Olmos) took a class of marginally motivated misfits from basic math to calculus in two years. In reality, those basic math students were long gone by the time he added calculus to the Garfield HS curriculum. It was his vision, but he didn't do it alone; he became department chair and hired teachers who helped him bring that academic culture to the school. None of this in any way diminishes his contribution or his teaching talent—in some ways, it is more impressive. Nor is it a reason not to learn from the example of Escalante—his engaging style and his relentless commitment. But he was not the miracle worker that I and probably many other aspiring educators were led to believe we could and should be.

Erin Gruwell, depicted in the movie *Freedom Writers*, has also offered us an example of inspired teaching. Her compassion, insight, dedication, and hard work helped students that others had given up on turn their lives around. As with *Stand and Deliver*, out of cinematic necessity, timelines were compressed. Also, according to some people associated with Long Beach Wilson HS, there were distortions about the school's overall socioeconomics and the neighborhood surrounding the school. Not at all a misrepresentation of the remarkable work Ms. Gruwell accomplished but a reason no beginning teacher ought to be disappointed in themselves if they cannot replicate what they saw on the screen.

The Subtleties of Teaching Aren't Very Cinematic

Along with the instant miracle worker teacher are many other familiarities of the dramatized classroom.

There is the prototypical out-of-control class in which students ignore or ridicule the teacher, make wise-cracks, throw things, etc. Like all clichés, it is rooted in truth. Most educators have seen—if not directly experienced—such a class. What we don't see on the screen is the complexity and uniqueness of the student cohort. One of the shortcomings of many inexperienced teachers—and some experienced teachers, actually—is an inability, especially during the most stressful moments, to see each student. The hard-to-manage class becomes a single tentacled monster, but a classroom of teenagers is a crowd of individuals, each needing to be seen and heard and wanting someone to somehow show they care and offer them some semblance of momentary structure and security. Accomplishing that might be the most challenging part of being a teacher, but there are ways and with time we can get pretty good at it. In the meantime, when we are struggling with unpleasant behavior, we must always avoid lumping kids together. The moment we negate their individuality, we lose them.

Another false implication often conveyed in these depictions of rude students tormenting the teacher is that such student behavior is by nature destructive and that good teachers must somehow control it. Some of the most powerful teaching comes when we are no longer afraid of the class descending into chaos, or, even, when we are able to embrace and nurture the chaos and guide it in a constructive direction. My favorite example of this from my own teaching happened during the distance learning of the Covid-19 pandemic when a class of 35 students started all shouting at once into the Zoom call and blowing up the chat box and I found myself suddenly filled with that joy of teaching kids that had been muted in the remote learning environment.

Not to say that teachers should lower behavioral expectations but schools often lean way too far into repression in the interest of order, and teachers, especially new ones, feel immense pressure to control students—and many depictions of high school classrooms reinforce those myopic preconceptions. I suppose someone could make a movie that shows all this, but until someone does, teachers should be wary of the dramatizations we've been fed about teaching.

Movies and television shows often give us high school classes as set pieces where discussions, lectures, confrontations, and mischief flow seamlessly with wit and intention, advancing plot, revealing character, expressing theme and, of course, entertaining the audience.

Dramatizations of teaching romanticize. They sentimentalize. They exaggerate, sometimes wildly, and indulge the fantasies of their creators and the fantasies of the audience. Like many of my colleagues, I enjoy watching these depictions of what I do. To whatever degree they ever come close to representing our work, they are almost always validating. And they aren't ever made for the purposes of training aspiring educators.

The real work of teaching is about incremental progress. Faith in our students and ourselves and paying our dues in the mundanity of planning and reflection, limitless empathy and endless patience. Our accomplishments can be monumental but are often imperceptible—and not at all cinematic—and sometimes the fruits of our labor don't materialize in our students for years.

> The real work of teaching is about incremental progress.

For me, becoming a teacher was humbling beyond anything I imagined. In some ways, it still is. It is raw and always imperfect and can sometimes, without warning, bring us to tears of joy and sorrow.

Unlike the actors who represent us for the cameras and then move on to the next role, teaching is about the long haul. It is endurance and toughness. It is the commitment to help our students carry their struggles. It is an unwavering belief in them until they can believe in themselves.

3

Teenagers Are Teenagers

In the summer of 2013, I was hired by the Harlem Village Academy in New York City to supervise and advise brand-new teachers in a summer school credit recovery program. I was in my mid-50s, yet I found myself, on quite a few occasions, explaining the behavior, the psychology, and the sensibilities of teenagers to aspiring educators in their twenties—some just out of college and only four or five years removed from high school!

Actually, there is nothing surprising in that. High school is a time of perpetual reinvention fraught with stress and trauma. Most of us endure those struggles without much perspective, then stagger into adulthood without much desire to look back—not at least until we have enough distance to become nostalgic and idealize the whole disaster.

So it is easy, during our first few years as teachers, to find ourselves caught off-guard by our students.

It's Not Pretty

Caught in a perpetual cycle of crises—many self-inflicted—as their bodies metamorphize, making sudden demands on them, they may only vaguely understand while spells of fatigue consume them and irritability along with sexual urges egg on new and often intense insecurities, teenagers often find themselves flailing in emotional angst.

DOI: 10.4324/9781003538936-5

It is no wonder that some of them seem so rude and inconsiderate. They can be extremely self-involved—and for good reason—as they try to construct an adult person out of the remnants of their childhood and their somewhat confused notions about themselves and the crazy world around them.

We can help them—sometimes more than parents, on whom they may feel too dependent. We can help them a lot more if we can avoid taking their sullenness personally.

Don't Expect Nice

Teenagers actually can be extremely nice people—sometimes even with sincerity and no ulterior motive—but I have found it highly useful never to count on it. Students will turn on us suddenly for their own survival. They lie to their parents, to a teacher's detriment, in order to explain a poor grade or some other misdemeanor. Years ago, I caught some boys staging a boxing tournament in the accessible bathroom stall, and they told the principal I'd been there the entire time and that I was holding the bets! They eventually capitulated and let me off the hook, but none of them apologized until years later when I ran into one of the pugilists, and we had some laughs about it.

What Might Bother Us About Them Bothers Them More

Teenagers have a low tolerance for boredom. They are often frustrated and cannot always articulate why. They are sometimes at the mercy of emotions they don't entirely understand. Some of this is physical. Their bodies are still growing. Their brains are still developing and their minds are in a constant state of restructuring. Without warning, their ways of thinking get rendered obsolete, and they are left in a kind of cognitive free fall.

They rarely get much sympathy for any of this. Their peers will sometimes seek to rise above their own confusion and torment by ridiculing each other. Sympathetic adults tend to be in short supply. Adult contempt for teenagers is perpetual.

> The only hope for many of them is a teacher who understands and cares.

We envy their youth and mock what we see as selfishness and stupidity. The fortunate teenagers have loving family members and loyal friends who still appreciate and accept them. Many have neither. The only hope for many of them is a teacher who understands and cares.

Impulse control is not a strength for teenagers. They desperately need external structure and resent us for creating it. They are aware that most adults find them annoying, and if you embrace their shortcomings and find ways to appreciate them anyway, they will appreciate you—though they won't always show it. They hear a lot of adult anger and disapproval in school and some also hear it at home. They will almost always respond to positive words and actions, especially from an adult, once they feel they can trust us.

Teenagers Are Contradictions

They want to be left alone and they want our undivided attention; they hate being told what to do and are lost without direction; they want desperately to be adults and are terrified of the prospect.

> What's most important for us is to understand that they want to learn.

What's most important for us is to understand that they want to learn. Let me repeat that—*they want to learn*. All of them, though many will scarcely admit it.

If you are anything like I was as a new teacher, you might find this claim completely absurd. Am I telling you that those students in that afternoon class, who can barely keep their heads up and their eyes open or stay off their phones or keep their hands to themselves, actually want to learn what you are trying to teach them?

Yes, I am, and it took me years to fully understand that and see past the seemingly endless resistance. Their fatigue and annoyance is real, but they want us to push them past it.

They want us to make them do the hard work of learning to read with depth, to understand and remember complex content and synthesize and calculate and write compellingly with clarity and an original voice. They may complain endlessly and mock our persistence, but they want tireless and determined teachers who believe in them. And, whether they ever admit it or not, they appreciate our commitment to their learning.

Pretend if You Have to

They need us to believe in them. At least they need to believe that we believe in them. Some teenagers already believe in themselves. Many do not. Those are the kids on whom we can have the greatest impact. Early in my career I sometimes caught myself thinking a kid was hopelessly lost in the cycle of poverty or gang violence or just their own recalcitrance. Thankfully I had the good sense to act as if I could see their path to success, and many of them showed me they could somehow find it. I still remember the names of those students who taught me that no kid is helpless or hopeless.

Facing a room of teenagers—angry or anxious, exhausted, and exasperated, and seeing all hope and possibility in their futures—is an act of faith.

Those kids are hoping, always, consciously or not, that someone will believe in them.

That is their act of faith—in us.

Part II
Getting Your Groove
Effective Teaching Is Affective Teaching

4
Develop Your Brand

My first day as a student teacher was almost my last. I was sent to a challenging school with a high population of at-risk students, mostly from South Los Angeles. It was just a few months before the civil unrest there following the acquittal of the four police officers seen clubbing Rodney King on videotape, but none of that was what caused me to nearly jettison the whole endeavor. It was one of the teachers with whom I'd been assigned to work.

Nancy Sands was a sweet middle-aged woman. Her warmth was infectious.

I felt it immediately upon meeting her. She was supportive and attentive toward me, and I quickly saw how her same nurturing qualities worked on the ninth-grade students in her room. She was like that mother of a friend who is your second mom, and I watched the effect she had on these tough and troubled kids. It was inspiring—and, for me, discouraging, because I didn't think I could ever relate to those kids like that.

Fortunately, I was also assigned to work with two teachers, and the other was Ann-Marie Powledge. She met me in the faculty lunchroom before the fifth-period class I was supposed to student teach and introduced me to a bunch of old colleagues who affectionately mocked me for wanting to be a teacher. She told them to shut up, then turned to me and asked me why the hell I wanted to be a teacher. I don't know if she and her colleagues understood just how reassuring their taunts were for me. They completely changed my mood. Then the bell rang, and I watched

Ann-Marie holler at kids about hurrying to their next class, then ask, "So, what's next period?" And after I told her, she seemed to be concocting the lesson in her head as we walked. I watched her work the room full of students, improvising a discussion, getting to know the kids, and instead of introducing me formally, she brought me into the discussion organically. Then she pulled copies of "A Clean, Well-Lighted Place" from a drawer and had me help her hand them out. By the end of the class, kids had read and were writing about the Hemingway short story. They were asking both of us for help explaining things, and I was thinking, with profound relief, *yes, I can do this.*

It was, of course, a rough semester for me of small failures and even smaller successes. Ultimately, I learned as much from earnest Nancy Sands as I did from sardonic shoot-from-the-hip Ann-Marie Powledge.

By the time they were done with me, I had begun to find myself as a teacher.

You Do You

There is no one way to achieve success as a teacher but one characteristic I believe all effective teachers share is this: a style and personality that is authentic to who they are.

That idea has not always been supported by schools or school systems or those in charge of them. I remember being told that the so-called education leaders wanted interchangeability. They wished to be able to shuffle resources throughout a school district without disruption. At one point, they even promoted the absurd idea that every class of Chem A or US History B or American Lit should be doing the exact same lesson every day in every school throughout the city. They said it was to accommodate the large population of transient students who, because of poverty and family instability, might change schools multiple times a year. A noble proposition to be sure, to focus on the most marginalized children. But I doubt it would have helped anyone, including those kids. If the district had actually been able to implement it, they would have managed to drain the life out of every class in every school. The same would be true if they got us all to suppress our individuality as teachers and become those interchangeable parts. Such impulses are indicative of the power struggle between those in education who make the big decisions and those of us who do the actual work of educating children. Our individual talents and the connections we make with our students are the keys to the institutional objectives and are not really within the control of those in charge—a flaw in the education system I will address in more depth in the book's final chapter.

For now, suffice it to say that teaching is an art as well as a science. Research can help us understand, in a general way, how students learn and what can produce positive outcomes for them. But on a Monday morning or a Friday afternoon—or pretty much any other time of any school day—all the variables, emotional, physical, economic, and social, are far more influencing factors than we can imagine, and many of them are not positive. We've got to be able to bring that A-game and an undeniable style born of knowledge of the subject, passion for teaching it, and some understanding of the kids and how they learn. Our students need to know who we are as teachers. Teenagers are especially sensitive to insincerity. Some will call it out. Others will simply be reluctant to trust a teacher they think is fake.

> Teaching is an art as well as a science.

Effective teachers aren't executing a formula. Yes, we are informed to some degree by the findings of experts but always as a response to the needs—intellectual and affective—of the students in the room. Effective teaching comes out of the connections we create between us and students, between students and their peers, between the subject matter and the students' lives. We are not likely to connect with our students or create an environment in which they connect with each other if we are not being some version of our authentic selves. Effective teaching is affective teaching.

> Effective teaching is affective teaching.

An Evolving Process

Developing our teaching style, our brand, and becoming who we are as teachers is an ongoing journey. It is informed by our students, our observations of them and the interactions we have with them; it is informed by self-reflection and the positive influences of successful colleagues.

I am not the same teacher I was ten or 20—and certainly not 30—years ago, and after more than three decades, I am still evolving. When I was new and impatient to find myself as a teacher, I borrowed a lot, imitated even, the styles of a few teachers I admired. I still do, sometimes, and I encourage you to be open to doing so, but never to lose track of who you are. The teenagers in our classes are doing the very hard work of forming their adult identities and sensibilities, and our own identity journeys can inspire them.

Each of us can offer students our knowledge and understanding of the world, our interests and passions, our experience of learning and failing and learning from those failures. Such openness is, of course, not obligatory. We are professionals entitled to as much privacy as we wish to have. You can share a lot less about yourself than I do and be a great teacher.

Play to Your Strengths and Knowledge

However open we are with students, they will learn about us and learn from what they learn about us. They observe and recognize from our strengths and challenges. Those of us who are really organized and thorough in all our preparations are offering students the opportunity to absorb some of that. Some of us who are most effective being as spontaneous as possible, have that to offer. Some of us are naturally outgoing. Some of us are more laid back. Some are serious-minded, and some of us are jokesters by nature. And everything in-between. I say lean into all of that.

And lead with your passion for the subject you are teaching. Never expect the enthusiasm to come from students. Maybe it will and we can even feign disappointment that students aren't as jazzed as we are about the genius of the Pythagorean Theorem or the beautiful logic of a balanced equation, the heroism of soldiers and revolutionaries, or the ways in which a story's plot, character, and theme all intersect. But we must always generate enough enthusiasm to fill the room and keep it going until it becomes at least a little infectious.

The Strauss Brand

My first impulse as a new teacher with students who had seen two others quit on them was to let students decorate the room. Give them ownership of the room, and they would see that I was for real, but students were uninspired by the idea, and why would they be if they suspected I wouldn't last either.

Instead, I started putting some of myself on the walls of the classroom in the hope that would signal my commitment to them. I don't remember everything I stuck to those walls. I tacked up some jazz posters and portraits of musicians and athletes who were my heroes. I hung color photocopies of impressionist paintings and Escher sketches, along with some tips for writing well. I don't know how much of that meant anything to any students. The only thing any of them ever commented on were photos of my family, especially one in which I was standing on our front lawn between my daughter, Carly, in a blue dress and our dog who we had gotten into Carly's matching red dress. I held Carly's hand and Tramper's paw and, if kids didn't look closely, I would hear them say, "Which daughter is that?" Then look again and realize, with great amusement, what they were looking at. That photo, taped to the side of a file cabinet, may have earned me as much cred with many of those kids as anything else I did that first year.

The teacher I tried to present to those students was one who was tough and caring and funny. I don't know how tough they believed I was or how much that mattered. The caring part was easy. As for funny, I had done standup in my early 20s and still had the timing and sensibility, and anyway the expectations were much lower for students stuck in a class than for paid customers in a comedy club. Mostly, the kids appreciated that I at least tried to be a little entertaining. They enjoyed mocking my lamest attempts at humor. I think the most important aspect of my brand as a teacher, though, was that I prioritized keeping students interested by giving them assignments that felt urgent and the learning objectives always tied in some way to their lives. It didn't always work, but the kids seemed to appreciate my effort, and when a lesson really bombed, I'd try really hard not to, even in my mind, blame it on the kids. In my best moments, I actually apologized for my teaching blunders.

My teaching style has evolved a lot since then. It has benefited from the influence of countless colleagues who have, by their example, helped me sharpen my instructional game in every way. I've actually become more organized than I ever imagined being about anything, and I'm probably funnier now than when I was performing at the Comedy Store. Mostly, I use humor to get the students' attention and help them cut through the myriad distractions in their lives and all the noise spewing from their phones.

I no longer care if I am perceived as tough. The walls of my classroom are a far more accurate reflection of my sensibilities as a teacher and as a person. On them are the not-so-absurd words of the absurdist playwright, Samuel Beckett: "EVER TRIED. EVER FAILED. NO MATTER. TRY AGAIN. FAIL AGAIN. FAIL BETTER." Very sound advice, especially for high school students learning how to write effectively and any teacher trying to help them.

The walls are also covered with vocabulary I think worth acquiring, including some really good replacements for the often-overused profanity. The only posted rules in my classroom are three words, each encircled with a line through it.

When I first posted NO CLICHÉS, some student would invariably ask, "What are kli-tchis?" Now, they know how to say the word and even how to detect them in their writing.

NO SELFIES is just me being a grouchy old man who, on a recent family vacation to Paris, saw the horror of tourists in the *Louvre* taking selfies with the Mona Lisa.

NO FLIRTING is a tactic. If two students are talking to each other when they shouldn't be, I just look at them and point to the sign and they get quiet.

Most of the rest of the wall space is for students—exemplary writing and student art. I'm not an art teacher except that we all are to some degree and the more the better, so long as it's appropriate. Student sketches—including a few cartoonish depictions of my bald head—hang all over the place, a free-for-all gallery.

Now, instead of wondering if I'll really be their teacher for the whole year, they wonder when this old man will retire.

What has evolved the most for me is my temperament and teaching style. I cannot remember the last time a classroom of students has gotten me frustrated or angry. They do sometimes try, but the only time I rant is to gush about the greatness of a work of literature or the importance of some aspect of good writing or effective argument. I rant about students realizing their own gifts and doing something with them, about learning for its own sake and not just the grade (though I fully understand why they are so focused on their grades).

If someone falls asleep, embarrassed as I might be that my class has rendered them unconscious, I poke fun at them. I pull out my phone and call it "the sleep cam" and photograph their head pressed to the cold desk and threaten to submit it to the yearbook, though I usually don't.

And I often play to my students' perpetual desire to get me off-topic. I let the discussion drift and sometimes initiate the digressions myself. I have learned that many students are more open to learning when it doesn't feel forced on them. Through these digressions, we quite often we find our way into very interesting and challenging perspectives. I have learned how to find ways to use the digressions to deepen the learning, and I have gotten quite good at carving a path back to the original objective.

I am, of course, not describing my teaching style to you because it should be yours, although you are welcome to any part of it you find useful. What I can tell you is that I am comfortable with who I am as a teacher and have been for a very long time, and that has made students comfortable and open to learning.

For me, this continues to be an ongoing process of renewal, reinvention, and collaboration with my students as they renew and reinvent themselves.

5
You've Kind of Got to Love Kids

Whenever the subject of becoming a teacher arises with my students, as part of a class discussion or in casual conversation during lunch in my room, almost without fail, most students recoil from the possibility and make abundantly clear that they would never want to deal with teenagers like them. Struggling teachers have told me about students asking them, "Why are you here?" and "How do you put up with us?" Which I believe is their way of saying, "Thank you."

It can seem, at times, that teenagers are driven by a desire to vex and that their ultimate objective is to send us fleeing for the exit. In fact, what they are more likely hoping for is proof that we will not, under any circumstances, give up on them.

> What they want more than anything is unconditional love and acceptance.

What they want more than anything is unconditional love and acceptance.

Even if they already have it from their parents—and many do not—they are hungry for validation from other adults they respect and trust. As educators, if we want to motivate kids, it is useful for us to be a source of that validation.

For me, though, the best reason to love my students, all of them, is that it makes my work much easier. I didn't begin teaching with that feeling. As a new teacher, I wanted very much to do right by students, but they seemed always to be a potential nemesis, more so than I'd ever imagined. I couldn't quite fathom they could ever be an ally. Not while so many were tormenting me, exposing the weakness of my inexperience and uncertainty. They could, seemingly on a whim, tie me in knots.

They Want Love and Need It, Most of All when They Seem Not to Care

My very first day teaching, I had students read a Larry Brown short story called "Boy and Dog," which included a description of a car exploding. I thought that and other hard-edged imagery would help win them over. Perhaps it did, but in any case, at the very moment we got to the exploding car, a young man named Ernest lit a firecracker. It was the perfect troll, really, for a new teacher trying to appeal to his wary students, an idealistic educator wishing to be inclusive and not punitive. I really didn't want to feed Ernest into the school discipline machinery over it—and as it turned out, no one outside our class even seemed to notice (blasts were tragically commonplace in South Central L.A. in the 1990s). Ernest said he was just trying to help bring the story to life. I thanked him and made him apologize to the class.

Other students in other classes had other ways of testing my commitment and patience. They pranked me with sounds from children's books tucked in their backpacks and drew unflattering pictures of each other and me on desks and on the blackboard when I wasn't looking. They threw up gang signs to see if they could scare me. Two young men named Jose and Carlos refused to do any work but would raise their hands every two minutes, and if I called on either of them, they'd say, "You're doing a really good job, sir." Some girls kept speaking Spanish and looking at me and laughing until the other bilingual kids in the class were all laughing at me. Kids would ask to go to the bathroom and never come back. Others would turn in pieces of paper with their name and an obscene sketch on it. Some kids seemed annoyed by the clowns and other disruptors, but I felt helpless to do much about it.

At times I lost my cool and actually learned a lot from that. The disruptors seemed, at first, to relish getting me upset. They giggled and mocked me (today, of course, they might try to film your meltdown). But there were also students who seemed upset. Perhaps they empathized with me, but more than that, I believe they were disappointed. They hungered for a teacher who was impervious. They wanted a role model of adult stability and strength, and after a while I realized that every kid in the room wanted that, including those who seemed to be doing everything they could do to undermine my teaching.

It is that contradiction that is the condition of many students and defines their ambiguous relationship with us—their conflicting objectives: reduce us to an emotional catastrophe that somehow validates their own suffering and the simultaneous desperation to overcome their suffering with the inspiration from our calm, our strength, and our stability.

Loving the Kids, No Matter What, Is an Affirmation of Ourselves

I wish I had learned these lessons sooner than I did. I believe that it took understanding my own fear and confusion in order to appreciate the fear and confusion of my students and to appreciate how their struggles and how they get through them is, as much as anything, what will define them as adults—and that, whether they know it consciously or not, they are counting on us to help them through.

Once I accepted the kids as they were, it became easier to accept myself as a teacher. Students were doing their best with whatever they had. So was I. There was no resignation in that; quite the opposite. Acceptance is hope.

When You Know You're Feeling It

There is a profound freedom in having that love for students. With it, there is little room for anger and contempt and frustration. The kids are no longer obstacles. Their chaotic adolescent energy no longer such an assault, and we can more clearly see the vulnerable child beneath the sullen or arrogant teenager.

I do not mean to suggest that I do not, at times, find my students exhausting. Just that the exhaustion is almost always equally invigorating. They keep me on my toes—which, as I have gotten older, has been exactly where I've needed to be—and I actually have come to thrive on that teenage energy and the challenge of helping them impose order on their inner and outer upheavals.

I did not fully appreciate this until the distance learning of the Covid-19 pandemic, when I found myself searching for the souls of my students with their energy and tumult through the tiny, mostly blank rectangles of a computer screen. In the fall of 2021, I had one class in which almost all 39 students popped into the Zoom on the first day of class. A few even had their cameras on and somehow, miraculously, they were loud and combative. There were arguments through the audio feed and simultaneously through the chat stream, and there were even moments when I felt I had lost control of what was going on, and after months of virtual silence, it was actually quite wonderful.

But I Do Mean Tough Love—to Go along with Idealism

Loving your students doesn't mean babying them. It doesn't mean trying to be anything to them other than dedicated teachers or asking them to be anything to us other than students. Sometimes, it means raising our voices and showing our disapproval and/or helping them understand that actions have consequences, good and bad.

> Loving your students doesn't mean babying them.

Most of all, it means being proudly—shamelessly—idealistic about those kids. That is how we can best serve and inspire them—seeing possibilities they cannot yet see in themselves.

There are students in every class who have been convinced, by the circumstances of their lives and the toxicities on social media and the misfortunes and/or cruelties of some of the people closest to them, that they are worthless. We can help change their minds, and that begins with making up our minds that every child is worthwhile and has enormous potential. Actually, it isn't exactly our job to do that. Rather, it is a means by which to make our job infinitely easier and more meaningful—to keep us wanting to get out of bed and go to work every day.

And I Mean All Students, Regardless of Who They Are or where or How They Live

I have often wondered, as you may be wondering now, if I would feel the same way about my students had I not spent my career with mostly underprivileged children in the inner-city. I hope so. I really hope so—and if not, then I don't know what I would be worth as an educator.

All children deserve the love and commitment of their teachers, however privileged or even entitled those children are. Providing high-quality education and comprehensive support to underprivileged children is a matter of social justice. Providing it to all children is a realization of the social contract and a down payment on our collective future.

Growing up is a struggle for all children, however well-off. Rich or poor or in between, they need teachers who care and value them. I discovered that way back when I tutored affluent kids in Beverly Hills and other wealthy enclaves around the western edge of L.A. County. Just as we must never dismiss a student as unteachable or, in any other way, hopeless, we ought to never ever practice class envy or class contempt as educators. If you are someone who sees excessive privilege as a social and economic outrage, consider that the more love and support a teacher provides the most privileged students, the less toxic their privilege will make them.

Whatever your philosophical beliefs, it is our obligation, and we ought to take that seriously.

The Ultimate Anti-Bullying Strategy

Love might be our most powerful teaching tool. That much became profoundly clear to me as a father. Parents see our own children learn so much so quickly during the first years of life, and we see that love is among the strongest motivators. Little kids want to please their parents and win their approval over and over. They listen to and watch us, and their total trust opens them up to learning whatever we teach them. Children learn how to love by being loved. Their intellectual and emotional development happen together.

That same confluence is true for the students in our classes. Our appreciation and love open them up to learning as we earn their trust and cooperation. It doesn't mean we still won't be subjected to unpleasant behavior or defiance or other symptoms of their mental and emotional turmoil. Quite the contrary. Some may actually trust us enough to present us the worst they have to offer, knowing that our response, however firm, will come from love and not contempt. But ultimately, the emotional investment we make in kids will earn cooperation along with trust. They won't want to earn our disapproval. Some of the kids we teach have yet to develop much of a conscience and may therefore seem only reachable through punitive consequences. They may appear to perceive love and support as weakness to exploit. In fact, while their condition may necessitate punitive consequences in that moment, feeling genuinely cared for and appreciated may be their only hope for developing the empathy and conscience they will need to be functioning adults.

Being loved and supported also helps children learn to love and appreciate others. Educators can reinforce the social good of those social skills, especially for those of our students who haven't always felt the love of a parent; but really any teenager who, as part of lurching toward adulthood, seeks to expand their role models beyond their parents.

I have seen it happen over and over and over—the more we care about our students, the more they learn to care about each other. Anyone, individual or institution, wanting to address bullying or homophobia or racial/ethnic tension in any form in their classroom or school, is wise to begin that effort with love.

> The more we care about our students, the more they learn to care about each other.

6

And Get to Know Your Students

Perhaps the best way we can show our fondness for kids—and become the teacher they need—is to get to know as much as we can about them. Listening to them, paying attention, and getting to know students, individually and collectively, should be the starting point of any teaching. There are learning objectives and there are standards to raise them toward—and beyond—and the most effective way to reach their minds is through their hearts. Kids listen to those who listen to them; they pay attention to those who see them; they respond to lessons that speak to them.

Anyone teaching in a public high school during the last 15 or 20 years has more than likely been fed a steady diet of student standardized test data. These scores, we get told, are essential reading and ought to inform our instruction. Such data certainly has its place and the reality that states, districts, schools, admins, and teachers are judged on them is reason enough to take them seriously.

But they are just one source of knowledge about our students. Even when they give an accurate snapshot of students' academic strengths and needs, and they do not always do that, they are by no means comprehensive.

Our own assessments and observations often provide us with more extensive and useful insights. Most successful teachers I know provide students with many opportunities, especially early in the school year, to reveal their abilities.

DOI: 10.4324/9781003538936-9

Kids are not, of course, the sum total of what they can do academically and how well they learn is informed by so much more, including their interests, passions, cultural and family backgrounds, and their emotional lives. Schools—especially public schools, particularly of the large urban variety—tend to be impersonal institutions. They regard students as a series of data points. Their average daily attendance finances the salaries of the professional educators. Graduation rates and test scores form the basis of how we are judged. Consciously or not, kids feel the institutional indifference to their humanity, and it can turn them indifferent to learning. Personalizing their experience, making sure they feel seen and heard, is the best—and maybe the only—way to coax them out of that indifference.

> Personalizing their experience, making sure they feel seen and heard, is the best—and maybe the only—way to coax them out of that indifference.

Ask a high school student what is good about their school, and they will tell you about the coaches, teachers, counselors, and administrators who have taken an interest, shown concern, made the effort to listen, and try to understand them.

If you are a parent, those are the educators you want looking after your child.

Student Records and Then Some

There is much to discover about the kids we teach; the more we learn about them, the less likely it is—or at least should be—that we will find ourselves misreading, misjudging, and miseducating them.

Our schools and districts compile a prodigious amount of information about students and require us to learn at least some of it, including which kids are entitled to special education services and what their individual education plan (IEP) indicate so that we can, as legally mandated, provide the stipulated accommodations (sometimes regardless of whether we are given reasonable means to do so). We are also informed about which kids are low-income and therefore qualify for free lunch, which students are in the foster system or are unhoused, and which students have been suspended or otherwise "disciplined." Such information can be useful, though we are wise to be wary of biases formed out of it.

Special Education IEPs, for example, are important legal documents with useful findings, but they can have substantial omissions and are not always updated accurately. I have taught students whose IEPs demanded special accommodations the student neither needed nor wanted. These are good conversations to have with students and can be the beginnings of meaningful collaboration with them. There are also countless students with special needs and challenges that have never been officially identified. We can make referrals but in the meantime it is up to us, however little or much special education training we have, to meet their learning needs.

So-called student discipline records can be particularly misleading. The circumstances in which students get into trouble are often highly ambiguous, and student defiance can be instigated and escalated by adult behavior. I have, on many occasions, asked students why their record includes a suspension or other punishment. Not to relitigate or challenge their record, but it is often interesting to hear their perspective and another meaningful way into student-teacher collaboration, which in my experience and observation is always the most effective way to get to know students.

Listen and Learn

However we are able to open the lines of communication, kids, given the chance and our interest, tell us a great deal about themselves.

As an English teacher, I have gained meaningful insights about students through their writing, especially when I help them write personal statements for scholarships and college admissions. I have read about the enormity of the pressure on some kids—to be the first in their family to go to college, to realize the dreams of struggling parents or live out the dreams of older siblings deferred by tragedy. I have also read about the emotional and physical scars carried in the hearts of students, the losses of loved ones to violence, illness, incarceration, mental illness, or substance addiction. Likewise, I have read about their personal struggles navigating unsafe streets along with the unsafe online environment to which almost all children are now subjected and the always perilous social world of modern teenagers online and offline. And I have read about their insecurities and fears and their interests and passions and a lot of their opinions.

Such discoveries are almost always learning opportunities; I often find myself recommending books, short stories, poems, articles, and films, and sometimes, such insights can be the basis of an assignment for an entire class since it is rare that the interests or challenges of one student are unique.

Learning about our students is just as likely to happen in casual conversation, sometimes just before or after the bell to start or end a class, or during lunch or other breaks or during the relaxed moments during a field trip or, if you do any coaching, on a bus to or from a game.

For me, the most meaningful revelations have emerged from my willingness to look past student opposition or lethargy. Early on, I learned to see student behavior not as an expression of their character or values but as a measure of their mood and temperament. A defiant attitude or a head resting on the desk can be a symptom of student adversity. Expressing concern and inviting them to step into a quiet corner of the room or just outside to talk can be a powerful response. It deescalates and even comforts a student in distress, even if the student doesn't wish to talk about what is troubling them.

Mostly they are open about it, especially when I remind them they are free to express anger or disappointment or annoyance with me. I do not pretend to be able to solve their problems—though I often have useful advice, which kids usually appreciate. Mostly the act of listening and caring is enough to make them willing to participate in the class and, if not, my understanding and patience is usually enough to get them back to learning soon. When a kid hits an emotional wall, the casual indifference of our class can feel cruel. For them to know that a teacher cares enough to take a moment for them means a lot and can accomplish a lot for us in building the trust and mutual respect that gets kids invested in what we are trying to teach them. Kids talk to each other. They know which teachers are their allies and are far more willing, even on a bad day, to support those teachers and the learning.

Am I suggesting it is most important to get to know our most challenged students? Perhaps—since it is often a more essential part of helping those students—but I am by no means suggesting anyone ignore our more successful and seemingly stable students. Pay attention to them and discover their interests and sensibilities. Be interested in them. Don't interrogate them. Let the conversation happen organically. Sometimes a doodle in the corner of an assignment can lead to a meaningful exchange. Or the song playing when you ask them to take out the ear buds or a book they are reading, or just the exasperation they express about your class.

It can be difficult, amid the hectic school day, to gain much knowledge of our students, but it is worth the effort and sometimes a little can go a long way. In time, the insights we do manage to acquire can help us better understand all of our students.

Deepening Our Understanding

For nearly ten years, I was part of my school district's corps of supplemental homeschool teachers. I was assigned, during the hours after school let out, to drive to the homes of kids who were unable to attend school in person, to teach them math and English and under certain circumstances other subjects. Among my students were kids recovering from car accidents and gunshot wounds, kids with anxiety and depression, cancer and sickle cell disease and other serious illnesses.

The work was challenging—sometimes heartbreaking, sometimes uplifting, always humbling. Being in the homes of students in the community in which I teach was enlightening. I saw tight-knit families in bright and beautifully kept rooms. I also saw crowded apartments—dark, barely furnished, hazardous, sometimes choked with cigarette smoke, children barely supervised by overwhelmed young mothers or aged grandparents. I saw gang activity through barred windows—a robbery, guns brandished at a car driving by—along with domestic disturbances and car accidents, one of which turned quickly to an assault. And since those days, I have never made assumptions about the kind of environment my students go home to. I know that while some have a quiet place to study, many do not. I avoid judgments about students who don't turn in homework or who appear not to be getting enough sleep. I try to find out what is going on and what I can do to help.

I experienced another awakening about my students' lives during the distance learning of the Covid-19 pandemic when I reached out to students who had stopped participating and were in danger of failing my class. Most apologized and promised to do better and none of them offered excuses, but I pressed them for explanations and found out what life was like for them at the other end of a Zoom class.

One student had left the state with his mother and brother after they were kicked out of the garage where they'd been staying; he was trying to log into class from a McDonald's parking lot with a Wi-Fi signal. The mother of another of my students ran a makeshift daycare in their tiny apartment, and my student had neglected my class in order to help a little boy who did not speak any English and couldn't follow his own Zoom class. Other kids were trying to follow class from construction sites and other places of employment where they were working to keep their families from catastrophe when parents lost their jobs at restaurants and other places of business that closed.

I believe many of us have a tendency to imagine our students' lives based upon how we grew up or how we've been able to raise our own children or based on some other very small sample. The more we know about our students' lives, the less we are prone to such assumptions and the better we can serve them.

The kids need teachers to share this information with each other. Not the very personal things they confide in us but the general understanding and all the reasons not to assume things about them when they struggle in our classes. The students who have the greatest challenges are often embarrassed by those challenges and reluctant to talk about them. The comfort of our respect for and confidence in them is a key to their success.

Knowledge Informs Instruction

It is difficult for me to quantify the degree to which knowledge of students can guide effective instruction. Knowing their academic strengths and vulnerabilities is vital. Diagnosing their deficiencies lets us build them a path to success. With experience, we become responsive to what excites their minds, what engages their hearts, and also what bores and frustrates them.

> With experience, we become responsive to what excites their minds, what engages their hearts, and also what bores and frustrates them.

The accumulation of what we know about them and their lives—their families, communities along with the culture of the school and the most resonant corners of the popular culture—should inform every teaching choice we make. When we explain things, we might find ourselves making analogies out of European football, a current rapper grudge, or perhaps some topic of student outrage within the school. The thinking questions we conceive might be tied in some way to a dilemma our own students are confronting in school or in their families or communities. We might end up designing entire lessons or units responsive to student interest.

What I love most about doing that is that it often emerges from students trying to derail my instruction and get us off-topic—as they love to do as a means of avoiding difficult work. In my class, that is usually some kind of close reading or analytic writing, and I will let things go for a while, let the students discuss and debate, until, unwittingly, they have created their next big assignment. A favorite example of this was a heated discussion about policing and police misconduct in communities of color. It was an emotional subject. Some students had experienced uncomfortable, degrading, and even terrifying experiences with the police. Others had someone in their family hurt, and in one case killed, by the police. A few had police officers in their families. The level of emotion in the room—along with all of the unresearched assumptions—all but required that I have students argue both sides of the issue based upon verifiable research, which could include interviews with people who'd had encounters with law enforcement or were, themselves, police officers. It proved a transformative assignment. One young man emerged as an intellectual leader among his peers, and his confidence propelled him ultimately to an elite university. The assignment influenced a young woman in the class to pursue a career in law enforcement as an agent of positive change. Nearly everyone in the class did impressive work and improved their writing.

At other times, familiarity with our students is just about a casual comment or exchange showing interest in them and respect for what matters to them. Those moments build trust and mutual respect that open the learning channels. A physical education and coaching colleague of mine always tries to figure out why a kid won't dress or participate in class. He told me about one young man who, it turned out, had wanted to play football but had some low grades and was ineligible, so he'd just given up on everything. The teacher asked the young man what his favorite food was and wound up promising him a Chipotle burrito if he dressed and participated five days in a row. The kid complied and kept going even after he got his burrito. He started enjoying class and never sat out again, and together they made a plan to get him eligible for next season.

Taking an interest in kids will almost always lead us to unexpected epiphanies—teachable moments that break through the monotony and malaise. I had a student I'll refer to with his initials, R.W. He was quiet and seemed pretty unenthusiastic about my class. He kept up with his assignments, but his work was uninspired, and I often had to make eye contact to get him to focus on what we were doing. I had really enjoyed teaching his sister and had promised her I would keep an eye on him, but he was a challenge for me. I could not seem to get him excited about anything, especially after his best friend got in a fight and ended up at another school. Soon after that, R.W. seemed to shut down completely. He put his head on the desk and wouldn't do anything. I invited him into the hallway and asked him what was going on. He told me his uncle had been shot. I expressed my sympathy and support and said I would give him some credit for the class if he preferred writing about what happened and how he felt or something else related to his family crisis. He chose not to but did make a minimal effort in my class after that, and I made sure to check in with him at least once a day to see how he was feeling.

After a few weeks, when I asked how he was, he told me his girlfriend had just broken up with him and he didn't know what to do. When I offered my insights and advice, he became very interested. When I suggested writing her a poem, he was open to the idea and motivated. When I printed out some Pablo Neruda poems, he read them enthusiastically, over and over, and marveled at how they conveyed the passions and desires and depth of love. Everything changed for R.W. as a student in my class. He understood the power and beauty of language, and that appreciation showed in his writing and discussion.

Most veteran teachers can tell you about teachable moments like this one and how experience teaches us to seize those opportunities and do the most with them for our students. Knowledge of those students, as much as we can compile from as many sources as we can access, is an essential tool in that effort.

7

It's All About Them Always

Teenagers tend to be self-centered. I certainly was, and so was everyone I knew. We were appalled by the self-centeredness of others, but rarely aware of our own.

It has long been a popular habit of adults to believe, with much derision, that young people are more wrapped up in themselves than any previous generation. I've heard those complaints from former students who became the parents of students in my classes, and I have had to point out to them that I remembered just how me-me-me they once were.

Somehow, they had matured out of it, as did my generation—most of us, at least, to varying degrees. It seems to be the natural course of human development. So there is hope for the kids in our classrooms, now and in the future. We can assist them with that growth. We can also more effectively teach them by understanding their developmental locus.

This begins with understanding and accepting their condition, transcending any of our own contempt for it. The stresses of adolescence can feel overwhelming. Their bodies and brains rapidly hurling them toward adulthood, while many adults—and our legal system and education codes—insist on treating them like children.

They must manage the physical demands of their emerging sexuality and navigate what they can appropriately do about it. They feel simultaneous impatience for freedom and autonomy, while dreading the responsibilities. Add to all that the stress we inflict upon them with our assignments and other demands along with all their parental expectations. Many also contend with poverty, fractured families, family discord, or alienation within their family (including that experienced by many LGBTQ kids) or the aftermath of sudden tragedy or learning or other disability.

Meanwhile, the clock is ticking and if they don't focus on themselves, they have little chance of being ready for the next phase of their lives. So if it seems they aren't thinking about anyone but themselves, it is probably because they don't have time.

Modeling Empathy

High school students can vary significantly in their capacity for empathy. You can sometimes measure it if you walk past a classroom with a substitute teacher having a bad day. Look at which kids are tormentors and which ones are not; the latter are probably the more empathetic, but we can help all our students further develop their empathy and concern for others.

The most effective way I've discovered for doing that is by making an effort to listen to them and understand them and to see things through their eyes. It is a way of establishing mutual respect and teaching empathy through example. It can be something simple, such as a way of reacting to their fatigue and disinterest in the class. I have told students that I would have felt the same way at their age. I have told students that when I have to attend professional developments, it sometimes takes great effort on my part to stay awake and engaged. I have told students that sometimes when I am reading, after ten or twenty minutes, my mind wanders, and that I have to take a break and come back to it.

Teenagers hunger for acceptance and validation and appreciate when they get it, especially from adults. They may not show that appreciation much less reciprocate the gesture, but the long-term impact is inevitable, at least for most of them, and in the meantime, making them feel seen, understood, and

> Teenagers hunger for acceptance and validation and appreciate when they get it, especially from adults.

appreciated can encourage students to stay focused in our classes. When they are at their worst—in mood and temperament—those are opportunities to show concern.

Teenagers want to fit in. They want to find their role. I learned the extent of that need working with kids who were trying to extricate themselves from the gang culture into which they'd been immersed through family or neighborhood. Aside from all the obvious perils of this endeavor, these kids had to reinvent themselves and create new ways of seeing themselves in the world. Those were opportunities for my colleagues and me to help them see themselves as students and potential scholars. It was hard work for them. Very hard. They often felt lost in their search for their new selves. Mostly, they endured and met the challenge and, in many cases, saved their own lives.

I also learned a lot about the intense power of identity from my experiences as a basketball coach. Those kids embraced the idea that they were leaders and role models in the school. They held each other accountable, in and out of class. Ironically, the most effective thing I did to facilitate the culture of accountability was to treat each player as an individual based on what I thought they needed, so I was harder on some than others. One young man, I'll call him G for short, had some emotional challenges. Sometimes, during games, he would have meltdowns and pout on the bench. I sensed his pain and offered him support and understanding. G's teammates didn't like that and let him and me know. I let them know that though I appreciated their concerns, I had my reasons, but then G walked off the floor in the middle of a game and I had to kick him off the team. He asked to come back, and I left it up to his teammates to decide. He confided in us that he'd been having a tough time since his mother, who was serving a life sentence for murder, had been moved to a prison too far for him to visit. He'd also had to change foster families twice that year. For the rest of the team, it proved a valuable lesson in the power of empathy. After that, they would often offer him emotional support. They seemed to understand that he was doing the best he could with the life he'd had to endure. I found out later that even before his mother's arrest, she had not provided him much love. She would leave him alone in motel rooms for days at a time with little food. His teammates might not have known all the details of G's trauma, but they understood enough to be moved by it—and seeing that helped me realize the profound potential of peer support and understanding.

Getting kids to understand and empathize with each other—especially those outside their circle of friends—is challenging but worth the effort. There is no special technique for this. Just a continual mediation amid the endless adolescent conflict swirling around our classrooms, pushing against their insistence that their adversaries—and sometimes their friends too—are stupid and mean as expressed via all the popular expletives of the angry moment. Often feuding students discredit me as an old fool, too generous and understanding for my own good, which I take to mean they admire my sentiment but just cannot imagine it ever being theirs. But it can be, eventually, as long as they keep hearing it. They can start thinking it even if they cannot yet feel it.

Sometimes I even dare to show my students empathy for their parents—even for parents putting unreasonable stress on them, parents expecting them to rescue the family from poverty or formerly incarcerated parents wanting a relationship the kid doesn't feel. I don't ask them to forgive or agree. I just tell them a little of what it is like to be a parent, with all the guilt and terror and awkwardness that can go with it.

> Empathy is part of cognitive development and abstract reasoning which students must develop in order to take on the academic challenges expected of them.

Developing empathy and becoming more selfless is a slow process. My motives are not therapeutic, and I do not suggest yours should be either—though if kids benefit somehow in that way, that's great. Empathy is part of cognitive development and abstract reasoning which students must develop in order to take on the academic challenges expected of them.

Classroom Culture of Recognition

In some ways, the most effective thing we can do about teenagers' preoccupation with themselves is to honor it.

Give them special attention or the illusion of it. With sometimes between 30 and 40 students per class, six or seven classes, it is unreasonable to expect ourselves to give anyone special attention, but there are ways to make a nod toward the individuality of the kids in our classes.

One way can be to casually or formally assign roles based on personalities and interests. Bossy kids can help organize activities and the distribution of materials. Kids who love to look things up are always useful—the word definer; the internet search expert; the skeptic—and hopefully, we have more than one of those. Even class clowns can be managed into something constructive through acknowledgment and a reasonable platform. I have even, in the last few years, found myself celebrating the documentarians in my classroom—you know, kids who are always looking to capture something on video for some social media channel. As I write this, my school district is plotting rightly to get the phones out of our classrooms, but I find myself contemplating the acquisition of a video camera, so the documentarians in my classroom can put their voyeurism to use as videographers filming discussions and presentations.

It takes time to develop the ability to work the classroom and make every kid in it feel seen and recognized in some way and what I recommend for the teachers I mentor is achievable goals, steps toward being able to do that, at least some of the time. Recognize one or two kids at a time for some talent or sensibility, or almost anything. I have recognized kids for their anger, the honesty of their bluntness, even—or especially—if it is aimed at me. Assertiveness and self-advocacy, those are qualities to encourage—even if, for the moment, they seem to be obstructing my lesson. A kid complains my lesson is boring, I might compliment their courage to speak out, tell them they might be the voice of their generation. Then apologize and promise to try and give them something better tomorrow—then smile and say, "Back to work."

Adolescence can be a time filled with aggravation and grievances, but most of the kids I have taught have not appeared to believe anyone much cared about what bothered them, and many seem unaware of their rights. When an adult does express an interest and takes the time to enlighten them on the subject, it conveys a high degree of respect and trust. We do well to make them aware of their rights in and out of our classes and to remind kids that we work for them—much as we might keep asking *them* to do work for *our* class.

Sometimes it is the little things that add up to making kids feel recognized and important in our classrooms. Making name placards out of folded over card stock is a favorite of mine. Kids can give themselves nicknames and draw icons of their personal brand and so on. I only have them displayed when students are presenting to the class, but I know teachers who hand them out every day.

> Sometimes it is the little things that add up to making kids feel recognized and important in our classrooms.

There is a reason that teachers are advised and often required to display student work. It supports the academic culture and provides opportunities for student recognition. I also hang up "quotable" things students say in class. Some because they are impressively insightful, others because they are unique or funny. Any opportunity to positively recognize students in our classrooms ought to be seized.

By making the class all about them, we provide students the space to focus more on other things. Our understanding and concern for them makes most kids care about us—even if they'd rather not. Our interest in them and praise for them makes them want to—or almost want to—be in our classes and trust the learning to which we are trying to subject them.

And of Course Connect the Curriculum to Them

Those of us who are parents or have spent a lot of time around children know that they possess natural curiosity and a hunger for learning. Those of us who have spent even a little time in a high school classroom have probably seen the apathy and lethargy that sadly seems to have replaced that enthusiasm. Why aren't students as interested in what we are trying to teach them? One reason is that as children get older, the match between what they are curious about and what we are trying to teach them can all but dissolve—our curriculums hardly ever address their most urgent needs or answer their most essential questions about life.

Language acquisition, which began for our students as an essential tool for communicating their needs and getting them met, can feel to them like a superfluous study of archaic rules. Their essential communication is by text or DM, the rules of which they could teach us. Nothing about geometry or algebra seems relevant to their lives. The biology and chemistry they care about is hardly taught and there is too much drama in their lives to worry about history.

Students with a strong academic motivation and college and professional aspirations often feel the urgency to learn whatever we say is important, but for most others, what we are offering is a distraction from what matters. Targeting our instruction at their social and emotional as well as intellectual and academic needs can give a greater sense of urgency to our classes and, at best, make learning a natural extension of who they are and what they want to be.

For teenagers, feeling smart and capable can be part of emotional well-being. Helping them understand complex and abstract material can be hugely validating. Whatever we do to bring the curriculum to where they are in their minds and hearts, it is useful to be mindful of their need to feel competent and the power of offering them even the smallest success.

My Subject or Your Subject

The idea of making the lessons relevant to the lives of our students has become a bit of a cliché and is sometimes overemphasized, sometimes to the exclusion of much of the valuable knowledge and skills they ought to acquire. Learning, at best, is a massive expansion of the mind, not a reinforcement of what we already know or a continual scanning of one's own horizon. Our job as teachers is to meet students where they are and take their minds and hearts somewhere they would not likely go on their own.

As a literature teacher, I find this a natural approach. Fiction and drama and poetry contain essential truths about the human experience—the vexing perplexity of relationships, the struggles for power, the ways that adversity test our character and define who we are and the myriad ways that conflicts with society and nature challenge us and inform our humanity. The lifelong endeavor to make meaning out of circumstance and experience can be well-fed in this way.

I began teaching with the idea that the literature to which I subjected my students ought to directly reflect their lives. I discovered it to be a useful approach that validated their lives and heritage and was more easily accessible, and as a new teacher, I needed things as easy for me and the students as possible. Since then, my approach has expanded, and I have discovered that all great literature can be made relatable to almost any student. In fact, it is often stories or dramas or poems from faraway places and distant times that have the greatest connection.

Teaching writing is teaching communication on a potentially essential level and self-expression in the deepest way. Students sometimes need to be reminded how essential that skill is—if they wish to be taken seriously in the adult world, especially if they ever want to earn a college degree or advance in a professional setting. Students often need to be convinced that they have or can have a unique style and a powerful voice. Most need a lot of encouragement, and all it takes is for us is to find one really solid sentence of theirs to legitimately tell them words to the effect of, "That is a great sentence. Simple, clear, strong, and distinctively you! Just make them all that good."

Give students a way to make everything they write personal. Even if the desired product is purely academic and objective, I tell them, for their first draft, to begin with how they feel at that moment writing it—a sentence or two that can be cut later, a way in through the mind and the heart. After a while, they likely won't need the gimmick to put themselves into what they write. There are English language arts teachers who teach writing as a series of formulaic steps; I do not encourage that method at all.

Knowledge and understanding of history and other social studies, is essential to our collective survival and the sustaining of our democracy and the accompanying freedoms and can teach students about power relationships and the most powerful influences in their lives and the lives of their families and communities. We can provide opportunities for students to understand the far-reaching impact of scarcity, the ways in which resources get distributed, and generally better understand the world outside the small circle of their lives.

I have collaborated and co-taught with history and government and economics teachers and discovered how the study of those subjects can begin with the students' perspective and experience. Having students collaborate on drafting their own Bill of Rights or creating a collective social history based on interviews with their own family elders and others in their community.

Teenagers are certainly fascinated with science—their bodies, other people's bodies, the chemicals they put in their bodies—and there is much they could learn about what they are eating and some of the health and other risks they are taking. They are curious about a lot of other science-related things, and all of it is a great starting point to get them to appreciate the urgency of knowing science and the scientific method. Not to mention understanding threats to the survival of humanity—climate change, the potentially rapid spread of lethal viruses and bacteria, the proliferation of artificial intelligence and robots and the pervasiveness of computers and the internet, the chemicals in our air and water and food, and the technology of the mobile communications students have trouble not using while we are trying to teach them. There are a lot of ways to meet students at their level of knowledge and understanding but also their level of interest. That can set up the biology or chemistry or physiology or physics to answer questions essential to these students.

Mathematics, too—no human activity is more vital than problem-solving. Computers and cell phones, on which we've all become so dependent, live and breathe sequences of numbers. So, of course, are the algorithms that are now so pervasive and onerous in our lives. Music is math. And there are an endless number of real-world problems with mathematical solutions.

On my last birthday, when my homeroom students found out my age, they asked me when I was going to retire. Rather than answer, I showed them a social security statement estimating how much I would receive at age 62, the amount at age 66 and 10 months, and the amount at 70. I asked students to calculate how long I would have to live in order to make it worthwhile to wait until 70 and was shocked that even the students who were passing AP calculus couldn't figure out how to solve it. Many years ago, our school offered a class in practical math, but the district canceled and then forbid the class, declaring that all students would graduate "college ready." A worthy goal, but I have wondered often since then why practical and high-level math are mutually exclusive, and I have seen effective math teachers who, whenever possible, show the potential practicality of mathematical abstractions.

Whatever you teach and however you decide to teach it, a good place to start is where the kids are—intellectually, socially, emotionally—and from there, create a path for them to learn. A good place for us to begin that process is to start where we are and connect our experiences and perspectives to our students. Every learning journey on which we wish our students to embark should be one we are willing to take with them—which might be the best way to ensure that we will be a presence in the lives of our students.

8

Be a Presence in Their Lives

Finding ways to connect with students in and out of class is a foundation of effective teachers and also a key to joy and fulfillment in the job. Taking an interest in what interests them, becoming knowledgeable about what matters to them, and finding ways to have positive interactions with students beyond the classroom are ways to establish mutual respect and appreciation with kids and to create a strong buffer against the fatigue and burnout that plague our profession.

How we make those connections can be a very personal and individual thing, and however we find our way to being a presence in the lives and imaginations of students, we are wise to remember that kids perpetually engage in the sometimes-agonizing work of reinvention as they stagger toward adulthood. This massive creative project requires an endless supply of role models from which to consider, sometimes borrow, even imitate, and often reject. Adults are potential materials from which they are sculpting their young life's artistic work, and so they are often more interested in us as people than in anything contained in our lesson plans. Resisting that may create unnecessary struggle. Offering them what is most useful can be a natural way of opening them up to learning.

The Cheerleader and the Salesman

I never had that knack for sales. I tried it a few times in my youth and was mostly awkward and pretty ineffective, much as

I admired those who were good at it, and when I was once offered an entry level advertising job, I declined. It used to annoy me that movies are promoted almost exclusively via the star actors with almost never a mention of the screenwriter who created the story and characters. It also vexes me that basketball is marketed via the star players to the exclusion of their teammates, reinforcing individual performances over the beautiful team sport that it is. I have come to terms with the wisdom of the marketers and have found it useful in thinking about what I do to promote learning—and, in a sense, market my curriculum—to my students.

I believe very deeply in what I teach, its value and urgency, but I do not expect my students to inherently share my passion for the beauty of language, the power of rhetoric. I do not expect them to automatically appreciate the profundity of subtleties and abstractions that are the connective tissue of literature.

I used to think of myself as a modern-day academic Willy Loman, a salesman with his sample case trying to close the deal on a poem by Walt Whitman or Nikki Giovanni or a short story by Garcia Marquez or James Baldwin or a scene from Shakespeare or Chekhov. I've become confident enough to no longer identify with poor old Willy Loman (though I am now older than that iconic character was). Still, for me, teaching is always at least part sales, and every successful salesperson I've ever talked to about that job has told me that you are always selling yourself, your personality, and your charm.

For the hour or 90 minutes that students are in my class, I am, for them, the face and heart and soul of the thesis statement, supporting reasons, supporting evidence and counterargument, the beauty of rhetorical efficiency and sparkling syntax, metaphor and subtext, and the intersection of style and meaning.

I am a sales rep for all of that and for words mattering and for reliable sources of evidence mattering and for the love of stories and books as well as great films and great music, and for pushing beyond academic success and the triumphs and agonies of the GPA and finding one's place in the beautiful continuum of human thought and culture, Western and otherwise.

For me, that often means not taking myself too seriously. It means being self-deprecating and at times self-mocking.

It means that when I rant about the deep meanings in the stanzas of Pablo Neruda or Mary Oliver, I am aware that I must seem to my students partly ridiculous but that I am also actually quite serious and hopefully, in some way, influential.

I am also quite serious about selling students on a belief in their own brilliance, their own goodness, and their potential to do great and meaningful things with, to reference Mary Oliver, their "one wild and precious life." I cannot overstate how important it is to sincerely express our belief in the kids we teach and to push them intellectually through encouragement.

I can cite many examples of how this has worked for my students. One I will always remember is a young man I'll refer to as G. He came from a middle school in disarray. He'd always gotten good grades, but the expectations had been so low and his classes had been so chaotic, that he lacked a lot of basic skills and his first week of high school had devastated him. What first impressed me about him was his focus and effort to understand challenging concepts. When he handed in his first paper, he apologized in advance. He told me he wasn't good at spelling or punctuation or writing. I told him not to worry about it, and my critique focused only on what was good. He came to my room for after-school tutoring and asked me to show him what was wrong with the paper. I showed him a few simple things. Didn't worry about structural issues or a few logic problems. I stuck with things he could easily see and fix. He became one of the best writers in the class and much of what had needed fixing he actually somehow figured out on his own. Two years later, when he was in my class again, he told me he'd almost left our school and even thought about dropping out that first week. He said my positive words about his writing had stopped him. When he said that, I realized that he'd gotten me to focus more on the positive with all student writing—he'd influenced me as much as I'd influenced him.

> How we cheerlead our students should be organic to our teaching style and sensibilities.

How we cheerlead our students should be organic to our teaching style and sensibilities. If it doesn't come off as sincere, such encouragement falls flat and can even alienate kids. So it is crucial that we really do believe in them. I have a colleague who conveys his tireless belief in his students almost entirely through irony—insults and ridicule his students fully understand mean the opposite—though I have seen him, in helping a kid in crisis, speak directly and earnestly. My own teaching style involves a lot of irony and sardonic humor, but when it comes to what I believe my students are capable of, an over-the-top fanatic for their potential. If they doubt me, I will attack them on behalf of them. "How dare you degenerate yourself! Not in my classroom! You can take that mess outside!"

I can also tell them, honestly and sincerely, that they are smarter now than I was at their age—and better writers—which is a very powerful message because I have managed to convince most of them that I am currently somewhat intelligent and reasonably articulate.

So the most important part of myself that I share with my students may well be that I was once a very dumb teenager.

Be Memorable

There are other pieces of my experiences and values that I share with students, many of them, in fact. I have, to illustrate literary or rhetorical concepts, told stories from my childhood as well as tales from my early years teaching. I have told students about growing up with a developmentally disabled brother and parents who suffered from alcoholism. I have talked about losing my brother in his 40s and about looking after my parents when they were very old and ultimately losing them and have conveyed some of my own struggles as a student and as a parent.

I am careful not to overshare. I am also very careful never to use my classroom or my students as a means to work out my personal challenges. What I share are things on which I have perspective. Lessons learned. Observations that I think have made me smarter and a better person. I do it as part of my efforts to put a human face on what they are learning but also, and even more so, as a means of always encouraging students to find themselves and their lives and those they love in the things they read and write about.

> Learning, at its best, is always personal.

Learning, at its best, is always personal. So I give students pieces of my mind and heart to go along with the words of John Steinbeck or Maya Angelou and everyone else I ask them to read, until students can connect pieces of their own minds and hearts with all the pieces left behind by those writers.

I believe that if I give students enough of myself, then my love of reading and writing and learning will always be highly infectious and potentially help students to become lifelong learners with love and respect for art and culture and ideas. The greatest praise I think I've ever received from a former student didn't come from one who became an English teacher or a journalist or a writer or who I helped get into an elite college. It came from a man who is now an electrician. He got C's in my class—and everyone else's—and then went to trade school. He used nothing I taught him to make money—which I think he makes quite a lot of now as a foreman on some pretty big construction projects. What he told me was that more than 20 years after high school, he still remembers fondly the things that I and a few of my colleagues taught him, the books we had him read, the films and music to which we exposed him. All of it has enriched his life beyond his work, and he believes made him a better parent and a better person.

As a new teacher, I often succumbed to the student tactic of getting me off-topic to delay the lesson and reduce their workload. I never fought it much. I found the digressions often became more interesting than what I was trying to teach them, and I mostly managed to keep it pretty educationally meaningful. With experience, I have become more skillful at controlling those digressions, and often I am able to steer the student ploy directly into what it is I am trying to teach. They hate when I do that—though, really, of course, they appreciate it.

It is those pieces of our lives, our thoughts and dreams, hopes and fears that keep all of us interested and connect us and emotionally engage us. It is what students remember most about our classes. Our students are trying, with everything they have, to begin the story of their lives. A teacher, whatever the subject matter, is helping them in that endeavor.

There is an important irony in all of this. The goal of a teacher with regard to our students—like the goal of parents with their children or therapists with their patients—should always be our own obsolescence; we want them to no longer need us. It is a goal we ought to be working toward with our students all the time and in any way we can. For me, the classes of which I am most proud are those in which I am the least overtly involved. When it takes a few moments for a visitor to find me. When I could—if it weren't against the education code—walk out of the classroom for five or ten minutes and wouldn't be missed. At the very least, when students do things without being told to or when students take charge of the learning and really make the class theirs. Some students are not ready for much of an active role, but all of them can become more autonomous in their learning; they can all learn to follow their curiosities and impose some intellectual discipline on themselves. Progress is always possible, and often over the years my students have surprised me.

This does not just happen. And it doesn't happen if we are not a presence in the room. It is our presence that provides the structure and security that allows students to take the most active role in their learning.

Extracurricular You, if You're Feeling It

The first few years of teaching can be utterly exhausting and the idea of running a club or coaching a team might seem absurd, but it is always worth considering. The extra time devoted to such activities can make classroom teaching smoother, and easier, and in the right circumstances, lessen our stress and exhaustion.

It can give us credibility and earn a little extra student respect that can go a long way. Becoming a basketball coach my first week in the classroom, when I was utterly overwhelmed, accomplished that for me. Suddenly, I found myself running basketball practices far more competently than I could teach a class and interacting with some of my most challenging students in an entirely different way, one we all found more comfortable. Bus rides to games produced opportunities for casual conversation that sometimes led to pretty deep discussions that became teachable moments. I redefined my relationships with the guys I was coaching, and it changed how most other students related to me as well. When a tough loss led to a post-game scuffle with an opponent, I had an opportunity to help a few guys who were on probation avert disaster. When the principal responded to a complaint about our team's allegedly "thuggish" appearance entering someone's gym, by requiring the guys to wear ties and jackets, the players and I further bonded when I taught a bunch of them how to knot a necktie. When the end of a short story we were reading in class made me tear up, several of the guys on the team got upset and asked me to please never cry in front of them again, and I got to make a statement to them about manhood and emotion.

Soon my room was a regular hangout during lunch, and I had many moments of casual conversations that became learning opportunities. When college applications were due, I stayed after basketball practice to help dozens of students with their personal statements and got much needed confidence with the teaching of writing. I began to think that the classes I was assigned to teach were really just the pretext for the real teaching I was doing during all those non-classroom interactions. And it did take a few years for me to believe the impact of my classroom teaching had caught up.

More than three decades later, an important part of my teaching still happens outside the structures of a class. In fact, I have come to believe that the word extracurricular itself is a misnomer. Anything we do with students—including clubs and sports, musical or dramatic productions, field trips, anything—any time we are a presence in the lives of our students can be a vital part of their education.

9

Some Focus on Fairness

High school can be an oppressive place for students. Self-expression and individuality are often crushed by rules conceived to ensure consistency, safety, and control. Discipline is often sweeping and punishes kids for the actions of others. Kids are uniformly treated with suspicion and even contempt, with their attendance, standardized test scores, and other data points prioritized over their actual well-being and growth.

Many kids feel alienated and dehumanized, and some respond with apathy and passivity. Others act out in rebellion. Still, others quietly internalize the injustices and sometimes arrive in our classrooms ready to fight for their rights or just quietly resent us for being part of their oppression. Whatever their attitude, and whatever their mental and emotional state, all kids appreciate any efforts we make to ensure fairness in our classes.

Treat Them as Individuals Responsible to Others

Managing a room with 30–40 students, and treating each kid as an individual, is extremely challenging. For me, as a new teacher, it seemed impossible. I could relate to each kid separately out of class, but when the classroom filled up, the students became a collective force of restless demands.

It took a long time for me to be able to identify and relate to individual student needs and interests and temperaments

DOI: 10.4324/9781003538936-12

during class. I tried to make small progress each day, increasing my reach a bit at a time. The greatest challenge was when a class became chaotic and started to spin out of control, kids off-task, grudges colliding, potential fights looming.

I remembered all the dos and don'ts my education professors had suggested for such occasions. Don't yell. Don't call out names. Command respect through posture and facial expression. Progressive consequences. There were days when I never quite got control. When class just ended in a pall of chaos and the room emptied, desks all askew, the papers I'd passed out littering the floor, and my relief that it was over soured by feelings of defeat and humiliation.

One time a colleague from a nearby room came in to see what all the noise was about. The first thing he told me was that posture and expression did not command respect, not in South Central L.A. He started calling out the names of the most disruptive students in the room and telling them to calm down. They responded, and later he told me how he believed he'd earned their respect: by showing up every day, trying to teach them regardless of their mood, helping them when they needed it, and by being fair. He urged me not to get angry at students or myself. He said that was an indulgence a teacher could simply not afford. And if I couldn't keep from getting angry, to avoid at all cost getting angry at everyone. They don't all deserve it and if you do that you will lose the kids who are the hardest working and most cooperative. Get them on your side and they might help you with the others.

What struck me most about that colleague's entrance into my classroom was that he'd only had to call out three names to get things quieted down. Once he got the attention of those three, the rest of the students went along. Over time, I developed my own techniques for getting students' attention. Sometimes, I would raise my voice but never in anger. I would do it with excitement or I would stage a distraction, pretend to kill an insect or knock over something by accident. Or stand at the front of the classroom and whisper and kids would start to quiet down to hear me. Ironic—or maybe not—that kids would talk over a teacher yelling for their attention, but sometimes quiet down to hear a whisper. Sometimes I would politely lean over to some students and ask them to help me get things quiet. They were usually happy to help. All of these techniques avoid the exasperation that tells students they are doing something wrong. It emphasizes an atmosphere of mutual respect and support.

Whenever I have had to admonish students, it is usually for doing something that could potentially harm another student, physically or emotionally. Or academically; preventing someone from learning ought to never be tolerated. I let them know that my classroom must be a safe place for everyone, and remind whoever I must admonish that I care just as much about their safety and will stand up for them in the same way. And always with forgiveness and understanding to go along with a stern reminder that they are part of a community, that they are important but so is everyone else.

I am all about them, but all of them, and in more than 30 years, I have only once felt compelled to report a student to an administrator for misbehaving. That student was being abusive to a peer, and I sent her to the admin because I guessed something was going on in her life that was making her act out, and the admin to whom I sent her was the person she was most comfortable confiding in. Otherwise, I have been fortunate to have been able to handle students in the room. Sending disruptive students to a dean or admin rarely has much of a lasting impact. Those non-classroom personnel have limited options, and the student pretty much always returns to class. Sentencing them to ten minutes or an hour with a dean or assistant principal or some other administrative type often does little to repair the student/teacher relationship. In fact, it tends to erode things.

The much more effective strategy of inviting the student to the doorway of the classroom or some other peripheral location is an opportunity for individualized interaction. It doesn't always have to be about dealing with a behavioral crisis. I have often spoken to kids about whether they feel well-served in my class. For those reluctant to be candid, I'll ask for their least favorite thing about the class. Anything to let them know that I am concerned about their well-being. For students whose behavior is less than exemplary, I have even asked if somehow I am the cause. Usually, they are flustered by the question and end up taking responsibility and apologizing. If a kid jumps on the opportunity to blame me, I'll offer an apology and promise to correct my behavior, which does a lot more to steady student behavior in the future than their own obligation to apologize or make a pledge. It also provides them a little lesson in humility and accountability.

Recognize Their Conception of Fairness, Then Broaden It

We are wise to realize, remember, and respect the ways our students conceive of fairness—and understand that it probably is not the same as ours. The morality of many teenagers is based upon what is right for them. You will hear it expressed quite plainly. "As long as I get mine," they'll say, or words to that effect. I remember when our school faced possible closure and some of the seniors, who were graduating anyway, seemed unable to share anyone else's sadness or outrage. Other graduating seniors, though, were concerned, mostly for friends or siblings in the lower grades—also typical for teenage moral reasoning. Only a few showed glimmers of a broader and more mature perspective—future kids in the community deserved to be able to attend our school. Kids do not get to that higher stage of reasoning by getting criticized for their narrow perspective. They develop by being challenged, compelled to think about issues of justice and presented with multiple perspectives, by being respected and appreciated whatever their thinking is, and by seeing their teachers make the effort to understand them and treat them fairly.

> Kids do not get to that higher stage of reasoning by getting criticized for their narrow perspective. They develop by being challenged.

Teenagers can get fixated on equality as justice and fairness. That is, of course, not unreasonable, but that rigidity can sometimes conflict with our objectives as teachers. I probably don't have to explain much about the concept of equity versus equality, a popular topic of debate among educators. Meeting the diverse educational needs of all our students requires at least some differentiation, and such measures can trigger feelings of unfairness in our students. Some students, for example, need more time to complete assignments. Some even have that accommodation recorded as a legal mandate in an IEP. So while we might determine that some students need to be held to strict deadlines, others are best served with more open-ended due dates. Complaints of unfairness should not surprise us. Nor should they be unchallenged.

For me, the key to helping students understand is by communicating and focusing the discussion on them. I approach such conversations with an open mind, prepared to renegotiate a due date, requiring that students think about and argue their own learning needs. Such conversations can be profound learning opportunities, pushing students to think in a more nuanced and empathetic way, and ultimately broaden their conception of justice and fairness.

Grading for Growth

I think pretty much all educators would love to be able to transcend the transactional nature of grades and somehow get our students to embrace learning for its own sake. It's a nice ideal, a cool dream, a reasonable goal but one that is unlikely to be fully realized. As long as colleges and parents and school leaders emphasize grades over the actual learning they are supposed to represent, so too will our students—and how we calculate grades will remain a sometimes-contentious issue.

When I was hired for my current job mid-semester, the principal handed me a mountain of student papers the previous teacher had left behind. She could provide no insight into what assignments had triggered these tritely self-conscious paragraphs, strange confessions, and seemingly incoherent ramblings. I remember weighing my options about what to do with them. I don't know why it wasn't obvious to me right away that if I tried to give these kids an assignment without acknowledging or in some way compensating them for the work they'd already done, I would be inviting resistance from the start. Why would they trust me to value their efforts? I had already become familiar, as a student teacher, with the intractably transactional nature of high school teaching—assignments = points = grades. So I cracked open the roll book I'd been given, handwrote every student's name in it copied from a printout the principal had given me, and started awarding points for the work some of them had done. I still couldn't figure out what any of the assignments were; so, at a loss, I simply awarded extra credit. I created a vague rubric in my head in order to translate their efforts into numbers that could be redeemed toward the grades I would ultimately give them.

The next day, when I introduced myself, I told students they all had a fresh start with me and that those who had turned in assignments for any of my brief predecessors would be rewarded with extra credit; those who had done nothing would not be penalized. It was the smartest thing I did those first days and weeks of my teaching career. The buy-in was immediate. I could see it in the eyes of the students—the power of what they perceived as fairness.

Since then, I have always tried to be clear and forthcoming with students about their grades and how they are arrived at. I always tell them that if they embrace the learning, if they can truly motivate themselves to become insightful readers and powerful writers, the A will be a given. But most students are stuck in the numerical loop of points and percentages that, for them, are the formula for success.

I used to tell students that I graded their papers and calculated their grades without looking at their names. I sensed the importance of their belief in my absolute objectivity as a measure of fairness. For many years now, my expectations for students have become more nuanced and individualized. I am always happy to explain my approach to students. I tell them I believe that if every student is given a path to success, they can acquire the skills and knowledge and earn the grades they deserve. Those paths need not—and likely should not—be identical. My goal is always to grade students as an accurate measure of growth rather than a tool for compliance, though there are times when the preferred option seems unavailable. Still, the guiding principle is to employ whatever will help the students improve their study habits, learn accountability, access the curriculum, and refine their skills. As long as I make it clear to students that my goal is all about them, then we have an understanding and I get little pushback.

In fact, the most pushback I think I have ever gotten was from an AP student who felt I unfairly gave her a grade *higher* than she deserved. R had demonstrated excellence in pretty much every aspect of the class—literary analysis, writing, critiquing, collaboration, and so on—but with a full load of AP and some community college classes she had struggled to keep up with assignments. On one paper she told me she had rushed and that it wasn't very good. It wasn't perfect, but it was by far the best of anyone in the class in almost every respect, and her idea of "rushing," it turned out, was writing it in less than two hours. I gave her an A and she fought me about it, said at best it deserved a B- but I wouldn't budge. I told her she could bring in her parents and complain to the principal if she wanted. I enjoyed the irony of our squabble. I believe she might have enjoyed it too. I gave her an A in the class, which she also protested, though after she was offered college admission and full financial aid to one of her top choices, we had a good laugh about how the A she hadn't wanted had helped her get in.

R is not a typical student, but she was one of many I have had the opportunity to help understand reasonable accountability and the relativity and nuance of fairness and justice, particularly in an academic setting.

Still, many students, especially younger ones, may not yet be capable of motivating themselves without impending disaster. They will test the limits of our efforts to hold them accountable. And, whether they know it or not, the system—prioritizing on-track students for on-time graduation—is very much on their side. I have found myself on many occasions mediating student recalcitrance for their sake, trying to help them discover academic discipline. Often this entails a kind of constructive gaslighting because in order to learn academic discipline, they need real consequences—but in order to learn from those consequences and not just give up, they need a lot of second chances.

One technique I have found useful is to provide alternative last-minute assignments that are much more difficult than the ones they could have done when they were due. A path to passing with at least some form of consequence. Not my favorite part of the job, reinforcing the superficial pedagogy of the carrot and the stick, and mostly the stick.

I would much rather spend my time getting kids excited about reading great stories and poems and developing their literary and rhetorical voices and their passion for art and culture. But it is hardly useful to worry about what I would rather be doing. The kids need us to focus on what they need.

Fairness, above all else, requires our own critical reasoning, an open mind and open-heart and a focus, as always, on what is in the best interest of each of our students.

10

Empowerment Is Power

Much of the advice about classroom management that I have read or been taught focuses on structure—rules and consequences, progressive discipline, and so on. Such approaches can achieve classroom control and maintain order. For students who have yet to develop much impulse control, external structures like that can be a necessary part of their development toward self-discipline. Such measures are probably essential for teaching middle school and, perhaps, to some degree, for teaching younger high school students.

I have recommended a variety of such strategies to beginning and struggling teachers over the years. Make students line up outside the room. Greet them as they enter the room, for example, and hand them an assignment, something to get them to sit down and work right away, so things don't get chaotic from the start. Collect that assignment in five or ten minutes and grade it right away, and do not accept it after that to coerce them into staying on-task.

Seating charts. Limitations on bathroom trips, etc.

They are a useful foundation for any teacher—but ought not, by any means, be the end point of how we conduct our classes. High school students are better off and ultimately respect us more if we can move past them.

I have seen too many educators get stuck in an adversarial mindset with students. It is understandable—especially when the culture of the school supports it—but it is not at all productive, not if our goal is to enlighten and inspire the kids we are teaching. I have heard too many discussions differentiating "good kids" from "bad kids." These kinds of distinctions are toxic. We are there for all the kids, and that means believing there is good in all of them, and they all have the potential to succeed.

For many of us, the first weeks, months, and even years of teaching can be overwhelming, even traumatic. There can be moments of helplessness and humiliation. When we finally start to feel that we have seized some control of our classes, it is natural to want to hold on to that control. What I have discovered, though, is that a teacher's greatest power comes not from controlling students but from empowering them.

> A teacher's greatest power comes not from controlling students but from empowering them.

The Sad Contradiction

It is no great revelation that most public high schools suffer a self-defeating contradiction: helping young people become adults by treating them like children and preparing them to participate in a democracy while ruling over them with an authoritarian hand.

Since the 1960s, some educators have tried to inject democracy into school governance and operation, mostly by including student representatives in important decisions, including budgets and discipline policies, but such efforts usually wind up being mostly symbolic. Some of the more ambitious efforts have included student-led student discipline arbitration. Despite mostly positive results, such efforts tend not to stay in place for long. They seem to produce too much anxiety for those in charge, whose power and control are diluted by giving a voice to stakeholders who will share none of the recriminations with the district or state if their collective decision-making leads to disaster. As long as admins are held accountable for everything that happens at a school, it may be a somewhat unreasonable to ask them to include students—or even teachers—in making important decisions.

So we have student governments that are window dressing, that neither plan nor do anything without administrative approval and have no real say in how the school is run. Famously, a few years ago, during his graduation speech, a senior class president (who was also valedictorian) at a high school in Pennsylvania began to criticize his principal for constraining his efforts to plan fun senior activities and the principal cut his microphone mid-speech. It made national news and the graduate got to finish his speech on the Tonight Show, but it represented all the silent disempowerment of teenagers in their schools.

Most of our students feel little—if any—ownership of the school. It is why custodians have so much to clean up, including graffiti. It contributes to truancy and dropout rates. It creates an undercurrent of student hostility that can get in the way of learning and that produces reciprocal hostility in teachers and admins. You hear it in the way many among us talk about our most challenged and challenging students. I have heard colleagues imagine some rude awakening due to a student they have come to dislike. Perhaps the worst outcome of this is that it reinforces the disempowerment of students and the idea that if we gave kids any say in anything it would put us on a slippery slope to *Lord of the Flies* dystopia.

I believe this is a tragic misunderstanding between us and our students based upon lack of imagination by those of us responsible for educating them. I do not believe it is hopeless or inevitable, certainly not within the walls of our classroom.

Student Drivers of the Curriculum

The most obvious thing we can do to empower our students is to give them a say in what they are learning and how they are learning it. We can discover their interests—by surveying them and by listening to them and carefully reading what they write—and we can find ways to satisfy those interests and connect them to the discipline we love and teach. We can find ways to let student passions inform our curriculum.

I have found this quite a natural enterprise with language arts. I caught two students distracted from the lesson one day reading about the news of a famous rapper charged with sexual abuse. By the end of that class, I had created an assignment using several articles on that subject. Students read them, analyzing the writing and reporting techniques of each, then formulated and wrote a paper on some aspect of the allegations or the reporting of them. When I introduce poetry to students, the first assignment is always a presentation analyzing a song or rap lyric of their choosing (within some restrictions for appropriateness). Some of my classes have asked if they can read one of my books. I am always ready for that request with a PDF of the novel, chapter tests, discussion questions, and various writing assignments.

I have seen history teachers take a similar approach, gauging student interest and from that tying current issues to events of the past. In an age of burgeoning scientific discoveries and innovations, student interest can also, tie easily the curricular choices. Math and foreign language may find it more challenging to respond to student interest, but sometimes a little can go a long way. I have seen word problems crafted or adapted to connect with student interest. Foreign language vocabulary can also make such connections. Watching news clips of high-interest content in that language can also help connect student learning to the world beyond school.

Offering students some say in what we teach may not be all that well-received. Not all students will immediately trust our sincerity. Others may have grown accustomed to their disempowerment and comfortable with it. Among those are the students who appear not to care about any of it. That sentiment was expressed to me during my first day as a teacher when a young man in an oversized T-shirt asked, "What do I have to do to get a D in here?" Apathetic or just wary, all our students are well-served if we persist in giving them a voice in the curriculum and some ownership in their learning. In my experience, students always ultimately appreciate our efforts to empower them.

Some of us have little flexibility in what we teach, students and teachers afflicted with uniform and even scripted curricula. In such schools, I urge any maneuvering within the strictures, pushing against that stultifying rigidity for the sake of student-teacher collaboration and student ownership. I believe that the kind of curricular homogeneity is designed to ensure a minimum quality of instruction—a hedge against teacher apathy or incompetence. These buffers of mediocrity against incompetence ought not hold back those of us who care about kids and the quality of our teaching. If nothing else, just the act of listening to students, seeking their interests, ideas, and feedback, even just a brief discussion to augment the fixed lesson, are well worth our time and effort. For your sake and the sake of your students!

Preempt the Power Struggles: Encourage Dissent

Arguments with teenagers are sometimes less about the subject of contention than they are a rhetorical tug of war, and it is tempting for teachers who find themselves engaged in such an argument to shut it down with a reference to our authority. We have the power of the grade, the phone (to tattle to their parents), and the power to get them in trouble with admins. We can also claim that our age and position are evidence that we are right or in the right.

I am probably guilty of most of these responses at some point but have discovered what, for me, has been a much better way to handle disagreements with students. I listen and take their reasoning seriously, even when I suspect that they are engaging in argument for its own sake. If I believe there might be educational value in the argument, I'll indulge it. Otherwise, I'll acknowledge and swat it down and move on, like this: "That's a great point. I think you should write a persuasive essay on it. I look forward to reading." or "Wish I could debate this with you more. You make some excellent points. You should have your own podcast." Such comments are not said with irony. The tone is one of respect and equality. There just isn't time to debate everything all the time—though I let them know that I am always available after class or at lunch and always happy to read and respond to that persuasive essay.

I think of this approach as addressing a student's assertion of power by deferring to it and sharing power, and by doing so, I let students know I am not afraid to surrender my authority and that I actually encourage them to assert themselves.

I no longer wish to have arguments with students about using the restroom during class. I am aware that students often disdain going between classes in order to hang out with friends. I don't blame them—and since the social isolation of Covid-19, they have every reason to prioritize socializing. Still, there are students who are chronically wanting to leave class and seem to stay out longer than might be necessary to relieve themselves. I ask them to pick the right moment— not during a student presentation or discussion or during instructions I am giving—and I sometimes tell them no. It is not a resolute rejection. More of a suggestion, and if they insist, then I remind them that time out of class will not excuse incomplete work.

I have, many times, allowed a student or multiple students to talk me into or out of something. I am usually happy when that happens—and, admittedly, often stage my argument intending all along to concede.

I have even left instructions for a substitute teacher to tell students they cannot work together on an assignment, and then to give in when kids pester them about it. The students are happy and cooperative with the sub once they get that concession, and I am happy to know that I have made students appreciate collaborative work by making them advocate for it.

In fact, a teaching goal of mine is always to encourage students to advocate for themselves, and I pay particular attention to the quiet and polite students who are less inclined to speak up and reward them when they overcome their reluctance. When I catch myself talking too much in class, I will sometimes ask a student if they would like to tell me to shut up. Some love the opportunity. Others cannot bring themselves to do that. I offer them a more polite and respectful way to request my silence. These are fun moments but also quite valuable for students. They are also an investment in trust and credibility for me so that if I ever need to take control of the room—if there is a serious altercation in which student safety is at risk, or if I am supposed to administer a high stakes test—there is almost never any resistance from students.

Otherwise, students are expected to speak their minds, especially when it comes to the curriculum. If, for example, we are analyzing a work of literature, my interpretation is just one possibility. I may defend its validity, but always with the hope that a student with a different interpretation will have a better argument.

I do not believe such an approach is limited to English language arts. As evidence based as science is, there are still points to disagree on. History, studied at its highest level, involves much interpretation. Even math comes alive when a teacher finds ways to inject ambiguity. And when the correct solution to a math problem is elusive, it can be a powerful learning tool for the student to argue for an incorrect answer and get other students to challenge it.

I have heard many colleagues over the years subscribe to that cliché that if you give an inch, they (students) will take a mile. That may be true about some things. Kids do push boundaries. If, for example, there is no consequence for coming late to class, some kids will do it more and sometimes push their arrival later and later. In my experience, though, that adage does not apply to many other power struggles. Kids need to develop their assertiveness. For some, that means getting the courage and self-esteem to speak up. For others, it means learning the power of politeness and respect. Whatever the challenge, being comfortable and effective at self-advocacy is a survival skill and an important part of our students' education.

Your Approach Will Vary

How you respond to student dissent is a personal choice. My style and methods have worked well for me, but they are not the only approach. I have mentored teachers who prefer a more controlled and contained response, but with the same goal of responding positively when students challenge them and making it a learning experience. You may arrive at a style that is uniquely yours and highly effective—eventually, if not right away.

As a teacher and a teacher mentor, I have found several principles useful for all teachers:

1—Avoid making a conflict with a student personal for us, even if the student is trying to. When a kid disrupts a class, they are harming their peers by undermining our objective. We should always make clear that whatever we do or say is intended to protect the other students from that disruption—and we would protect the disruptor if they were trying to learn and someone else tried to obstruct that. By putting it that way, we make clear that we are advocating for all the students in the room at that moment—including the disruptor. Our ego and vanity have nothing to do with it.

We are, of course, human, and no one likes to feel targeted in any way or devalued by anyone, especially the students for whom we work so hard. But as soon as our stance is one of advocating for students, we diminish the incentive of the disruptor and erode much of their peer support—even if that might not be evident at that moment. We should assume the same stance if a student directly disrespects us. If they disrespect the teacher, they disrespect the class and their peers in it. The goal is to socially isolate the offender with the standing offer of forgiveness.

2—Always try to provide an off-ramp for the student that enables them to save face. Kids have bad days and bad moments and make bad choices. Shame can be a tool for growth. Humiliation can be overwhelming and emotionally debilitating. Helping a kid transform an undisciplined outburst into a laughable lapse can be the most effective tool for their growth, meaningful also for their peers and for us. It is the essence of what we want to achieve as teachers.

There is nothing all that profound in that realization. Whenever we find ourselves in or approaching a power struggle with a student, we should recognize that it can produce an important teachable moment—for that student, for the rest of the class, and for ourselves.

Part III
Win Win
Success Is the Means and the Ends

11
Modest Goals and a Vision of the Long Term

She was 23 years old, hired on an emergency credential, and it was her first day as a classroom teacher. The summer school students were there to make up a class they'd failed. I was there as a visiting mentor and let this first day teacher know that I was there to support her. I might offer advice, and it would come entirely free of judgment. She seemed very nervous, and soon the students seemed aware of that. Some sneered and snickered, which seemed to intensify her state of anxiety.

She had meticulously planned her opening lesson but soon began to stumble. All very understandable. How can anyone know how to pace a class if they've never done it before? Especially if they know nothing about the students they are supposed to be teaching. I tried, with my expression and a thumbs up, to let her know she was, under the circumstances, doing great. She really was. She muscled through her uncertainty and seemed to adjust herself to what the kids were doing and not doing. She managed to get through the lesson and the students, if a little distracted, seemed to be learning. There were moments of student engagement, and some kids even seemed to forget it was summer school and might have been enjoying themselves. The low point of the class for her, I could tell, was when two boys got completely sidetracked and when she tried to politely get them back on task, they started whispering things to each other and laughing.

After the students left, I approached her to let her know how great I thought she had done. For a first day teacher, she really had. But before I could tell her anything, she burst into tears.

Fortunately, she had a break after that class and was able to cry herself out and still had time for the redness in her eyes to fade before any more kids entered the room. What I discovered in the next few minutes was that her pain stemmed from three common afflictions among new teachers.

Judgment Is Real and Not Always Constructive

To teach is to be judged.

Kids judge us all day—some like to scrutinize everything we do. It is a part of their learning process, admiring, critiquing, rejecting. It is part of their own process of inventing themselves as adults. A student in my class a few years ago sat in the back row and criticized me all year. She told me my assignments were dumb and that my jokes weren't funny (though I caught her laughing at a few of them). At a parent conference, her aunt told me that I was her favorite teacher. In my experience, though, most student judgments are the calculations of what we really expect of them, how far they can push our limits, and whether they can trust us.

Our admins may or may not be all that interested in what we do in our classrooms but they are required to evaluate us and some of them have bosses who will judge them if they are not critical enough of us.

At times, we will be judged by our colleagues. Some of that will hopefully be constructive, but teachers are human, and some are prone to grudges and pettiness. Most of us hope we offer a mature influence on our students, but they outnumber us, and some teachers are vulnerable to the influence of all that teenage energy, insecurity, fear, and loathing. Their influence on us is something to beware of.

Teachers are also judged, sometimes harshly, by the parents of our students. Some of it may be deserved, some may flow from parental protectiveness, and some can result from their personal baggage. As a white teacher in a predominantly African American school in the 1990s, for example, I sometimes endured the scorn of parents who had, as students, been marginalized and had suffered mistreatment by white teachers. It was understandable for them to regard me with suspicion.

Perhaps most burdensome of all, teachers must endure the judgment of politicians and the public at large. We are sometimes scapegoated for the deficiencies of students, dismissed as losers and broadly accused of incompetence and of plotting to indoctrinate students in some way or other.

We are wise to prepare ourselves for the onslaught of judgment and develop an open mind and a thick skin. If we are reflective about our practice and motivated to continuously improve to meet the evolving challenges, then we welcome meaningful and constructive criticism. The rest of it is just noise. Blocking out that noise and rising above it sets a good example for our students who are trying to overcome their own self-consciousness and its accompanying anxiety and depression.

> Blocking out that noise and rising above it sets a good example for our students.

Perfection Is Probably Not an Option

We all have our reasons for wanting to become teachers, and each of us brings with us the baggage of our own educational experiences. For some of us, it is the trauma of feeling stupid or weird or out of place, and for others, it is the alienation of feeling invisible or being bullied. For others, the baggage is the expectation of perfection or near-perfection that comes from having earned those perfect report cards and the praise of teachers.

Being the teacher in the room is different. It is way different. Teaching is an imperfect endeavor. It is a sometimes-impossible task. We inherit all the disaster of a chaotic and violent world, distressed and alienated communities, and the family dysfunction and personal trauma some children have had to endure—along with the general state of crisis of pretty much all teenagers.

Believing anyone can possibly fix it all is crazy. Feeling suddenly responsible for all of it is self-defeating.

We ought to have high expectations for ourselves—as we should for our students—but we also need to be realistic about what is possible each day. The better we get at teaching, the more we tend to realize the potential of our students and our teaching—and the more we have to manage our expectations. If we could work 24 hours a day seven days a week, we could do so much more, but we truly—literally—would burn out, and in that state, we could accomplish nothing.

> We ought to have high expectations for ourselves—as we should for our students—but we also need to be realistic about what is possible each day.

Educating teenagers is about progress and growth, and success is difficult to measure. Teaching summer school myself one year, I had a few students who seemed determined to fail the class again. They kept showing up but seemed unable, at times, to make the slightest effort. I tried over and over to get them excited about reading and writing, to make it fun and interesting, but I couldn't seem to get them to spark to anything. Part of the final exam was a self-evaluation and most of them said the class had been fun and interesting and that they had learned, but I assumed they were only saying that so that I would pass them. Most students seemed to spark to the class, but those few seemingly intractable kids left me with a bad feeling about that summer term. I didn't see most of those kids again since I teach at a different school during the regular school year, but the next summer I saw one kid who came to pick up his girlfriend and another walking through campus to football practice. They both thanked me for the previous summer. They said I had helped them become better students and they'd passed all their classes that year. It sure hadn't felt like anything close to success at the time but that is often how it is.

Idealists Need to Be a Little Realistic

Idealism is foundational to effective teaching. It is also a survival skill for teachers.

Our students do not always show signs of interest in what we are teaching or aptitude for learning it. Many do not believe in themselves at all and may or may not have families who believe in them. For some students, their only hope is our ability to imagine their potential and foresee their success, even when they seem to be trying to convince us that they are hopeless.

But idealism can also be a burden for us, especially when we begin to realize the potential of great teaching but aren't yet able to achieve it. I have worked with young teachers who questioned whether they belonged in the classroom at all, who feared their lack of skill—from lack of experience—was too great a burden for their students. "These kids deserve better than I can give them," they lamented.

These idealist teachers often don't realize how good they already are. They have an unrealistic idea of what an engaging and effective class is like. If they have observed other teachers, they may only have seen those moments during which teacher and students are trying their hardest and engaging the most. And, again, we cannot always see our impact on students right away.

The only way any of us can ultimately do justice to kids is through the learning process of experience. Like the Samuel Becket quote on the wall of my classroom. You have to keep "failing better" to get really good at this teaching thing, and students in five or ten or 20 years need new teachers of right now to endure that process. Our stumbles through trial and error are not only necessary but inspirational. It is what our students are going through in their own way. We can be role models for them of patience and determination.

And, finally, the fact that anyone is so dedicated to student success that they feel unworthy of those students is proof that they are probably destined to become a great teacher.

12

Bring the Passion

When I returned to college a few months after my 30th birthday—and after more than five years away from school of any kind—I discovered something remarkable: I enjoyed learning. Even dense texts and complex material and extensive writing assignments. Even when the professor seemed to be doing their best to make the class tedious and torturous, I could find a way to connect to the subject and motivate myself. The value of that experience for me, as a teacher, is incalculable. It reminded me how uninterested and unmotivated I was as a teenager and has saved me from wasting too much time and energy getting frustrated by the lack of interest or self-motivation of my students. And, instead, to try to convey endless passion for whatever it is I am supposed to be teaching.

This is easy for me because I love the subject. I get to share great works of fiction and poetry, brilliant plays and essay by some of my heroes. I get to convey to students the power of language in what they read and how they can find the power in their own voices as writers. The history teachers I see having the most success and enjoyment have the same kind of love and passion for the study of the past and its relationship to the moment. I see the same kind of joy and effectiveness from science teachers with that love and passion for understanding the physical universe and from math teachers bringing the same kind of enthusiasm to the complexity and logic of number systems and the profound power of what they can accomplish. The same holds true for music and art teachers, foreign language teachers, physical education teachers, and so on.

I am not sure why anyone would want to teach something they don't love.

Do Not Expect Students to Share that Passion

If students shared our level of interest, they might not need us. At a time when computers and the internet and AI seem to offer access to virtually all knowledge, I may only be slightly exaggerating. Our greatest value as human teachers, then, may well be our love and enthusiasm for the subject we are teaching and, with that, our ability to excite students.

Given that, our jobs seem pretty safe, at least for now, as most kids bring little enthusiasm to our fields of study, and we are wise not to expect them to. Embrace the complaining. It is part of the ritual.

Hopefully by the end of a term or a school year we have instigated at least a little excitement and interest in our students, but we shouldn't be disappointed or surprised if they remain impervious—or seem so. Remember that our impact on students doesn't always manifest before our eyes.

> Remember that our impact on students doesn't always manifest before our eyes.

It takes time also for us to learn how to spot the signs of our success. We cannot expect the kids to tell us—though some will.

If You Feel a Little Like a Doofus You're Probably Doing It Right

> Never be afraid to be the only excited person in the room.

Never be afraid to be the only excited person in the room. Get used to it. Embrace it. I think of it as if I am the only person in the room still breathing and having to administer intellectual CPR on the entire class.

It isn't easy to gush with enthusiasm while students gape and stare and look down or shake their heads. It is especially hard if we are holding onto any need to seem cool. I am not proud to admit that I suffered from that when I began teaching—at age 33!—but I got over it pretty quickly. My students were quite expert at humbling a new teacher. They helped me find the freedom to be the only excited person in the room—a kind of self-styled English Language Arts nerd. Ironically, my newfound unselfconsciousness made me feel kind of cool (which was perhaps the strongest evidence, of what a doofus I'd become).

Give and Take

Expressing unreserved enthusiasm in the face of student dispassion and lethargy doesn't mean we cannot be sympathetic to their condition. We were all once young and probably as impatient and self-obsessed, in our own way, as our students. Carrying the passion in the room doesn't mean disdaining their condition. We can understand their reluctance, their fatigue, and sympathize with it, and then work against it.

We can tell them how lucky they are to read Shakespeare or learn about the wondrous mysteries of right triangles or chemical equations or whatever. If we are relentless in our devotion to what we are teaching and our desire to impart it to our students, if we hold onto that love no matter how little our students seem moved by it, we will surely reach them in some way.

They may not show it. At least not right away. But at least some important part of our message will ultimately get through—even if only that someone cares and that learning matters. I have been visited by the most painfully uninterested students five or ten years later and told how much it mattered. Those visits happen every day to countless educators. And the message of those former students is for all of us: don't give up, don't give in, don't lose the love or the passion. It is never in vain.

13

Nice Is Not Weak

When I was a new teacher, someone gave me this advice: *Don't smile at the students for the first six months.* Someone else told me: *If you're too nice, they'll eat you alive.*

I'm not sure anyone says any of that to new teachers anymore. I hope not. Projecting strength is essential for new teachers and it is easy to believe that being too nice could get in the way. My experience and observations do not support that assumption.

I have long suspected there might be some confusion about what it actually means to be nice to students. Over the years, I have gained a lot of clarity on the subject. My insight on the subject may well have begun the morning I reacted to a student who hardly ever showed up and usually disrupted class when he did. He'd been gone more than a week at the time and came in the room late, demanding all the assignments he'd missed. I was already stressed from the effort of settling the class into their group assignment, and now I had to figure out a group for him. He kept pestering me about his makeup assignments until I lost my cool and yelled at him. I told him he needed to show he was taking this class seriously; otherwise he was a waste of time for me. The rest of our argument went something like this:

Him: You're supposed to help me.
Me: Yeah—and you're supposed to come to school.
Him: I'm here!

Me: Great, but where were you the last week and a half?
Him: My mom got shot. I had to help raise money for the funeral.

How was I supposed to know any of that? He was always missing school. Didn't matter. I felt awful—in a way I never wanted to feel again. Our students need us to be there for them—if not for emotional support, then at least for stability and to provide an emotional refuge, a safe place and some positive vibes.

The lesson I learned that morning might have been the most poignant one about my interactions with students, though I have since discovered other reasons to be nice to them.

Smiling Is Good

I actually did smile during my first six months, but only a little and with trepidation, wary of being perceived as weak and losing control of my classes. I had nightmares about classroom chaos. I'd seen teachers turned to virtual hostages, barricaded in closets, weeping in bathrooms. I responded to my fear the way I had as a 12-year-old kid riding the New York subways in the early 1970s—with a scowl I hoped would repel the dangers.

I imposed a strictness on my students that showed I didn't trust them not to make mayhem at any moment. I perspired profusely while teaching. But I had enough positive interactions with students to begin to realize how nice they all could be when they weren't in the heat of an overcrowded class, battling their academic and personal insecurities, vying for attention and peer status, and, in some cases, their street rep.

What I discovered was just how desperately they hungered for validation and even kindness from a trusted adult. I began to understand that their seeming cynicism and nihilism were mostly a posture against their own peril and that underneath all that they were still sweet kids. One poignant illustration of that presented itself whenever we read a short story or watched a short film and I asked them to either predict the end of the story or imagine what happened to the characters afterward.

No matter how grim the story or the tone of the story, their endings were always idyllic. It was, I realized, how they hoped—despite everything around them—that their lives would turn out.

> So I started smiling and saw how much they needed to see that smile.

So I started smiling and saw how much they needed to see that smile. Even in class, I would let myself smile at students. I discovered that they seemed to like seeing me in good spirits. Some of them would mock me for it, but I could tell that was only for show. My upbeat mood and the outwards signs of it were, more than anything else, reassurance to them that life could be good, that joy was attainable.

Interestingly, smiling turned out to be a net gain with classroom management. If I could seem relaxed and happy, it concealed my stress and helped me through it and reassured kids that whatever they were doing wasn't getting to me.

The Power of Pleasant

Being nice to students shows them that we are confident and that we trust them. It demonstrates a kind of mental and emotional endurance, an appreciation for our students, and who they are in all their imperfectness and incompleteness. It shows them that we understand the struggles they are going through in our classes and beyond.

Being nice to students who are not being nice to us—who are being rude or impatient, thoughtless, careless, indifferent, or even cruel—is a powerful statement to them. It says that we are professional, and we are there to do a job. It says that we are compassionate and loving. We know they are better than what they are doing or saying at that moment and that we are confident that they can be better, even if they don't believe that.

> Being nice to students is freedom.

Being nice to students is freedom. It relieves us from the burden of their torment. It can often free us from the torture of going down the rabbit hole of conflict with them. Being nice to students is disarming. Every student/teacher fight I have witnessed or known of—verbal and/or physical—(and there have been plenty over the years) began as a small disagreement that escalated. Being nice deescalates conflict. Nice also makes us more likely to really listen to students—and makes them more likely to listen to us.

I have been accosted by students who seemed ready for a battle, and I have seen their entire demeanor change simply because I was nice to them. I have also been tested by students who perceived my warmth as weakness and tried to push my limits and even intimidate me. But it didn't take much firm resolve to convince them that I was not intimidated and that I would stand my ground. Remaining relatively nice made the self-assertion easier, and I could still convey my concern for their well-being and helped create a natural path for the combative student to save face and reconsider their attitude and actions.

Being nice does not require deferring to anyone, though I am never afraid to defer to students when I believe it is in their interest. That willingness, in fact, is an expression of strength as well as trust and respect.

This approach seems, to many of the teachers I have mentored, radical and even scary. I tell them to do what is comfortable. Try a little at a time. Many teachers are, by nature, nice people and feel almost as if they can only survive the combat of high school teaching by playing the role with a posture of toughness and cool. It may be difficult for most of us to be nice without seeming—or even feeling—weak until we are quite comfortable in the classroom with our students. This is why getting to know our students is so valuable.

But it works. It really does. I think the teacher I am most proud to have mentored in this way is my daughter. She began teaching art at a continuation school with kids who were mostly reluctant learners, discouraged students, often quite oppositional. Initially, she focused on being tough while holding students accountable to keep them focused and learning despite themselves. Then she experimented with being nice while still holding kids accountable and was impressed by the result. Some students were more inclined to do their work, and most were nice back to her. When interactions with students became less stressful, her job became easier.

Funnel Frustration into Passion

I hope that I have not given the impression that teaching high school can be free of frustration and even some occasional anger. Even after all these years, I still get surprised by the sometimes-outrageous ways students manage to get under my skin. Fortunately, though, I have, for quite a long time, been able to avoid expressing anger or frustration directly at kids.

I still remember most of the times, early in my career, when I completely lost my cool. I screamed profanities at a young woman who wouldn't stop applying makeup or talking to her friend, and I watched her completely shut down and watched the rest of the class regard me with what seemed like disgust. I yelled and threw a piece of chalk at a young man who emptied his backpack onto the floor while I was trying to explain a homework assignment to the class. The next day, he imitated my tirade, including the chalk toss, to the delight of the class.

I do not believe anything positive ever comes from raging at students.

I have, however, found that if I am calm—and nice—that if I ever need to express outrage at them, usually about their mistreatment of a peer, they are usually moved by my uncharacteristic seriousness and severity.

I have also discovered that expressing anger or any intense emotion—when it isn't directed at students—can be an effective tool for getting students' attention, getting them to snap out of their daydreams and get interested in the lesson. I have screamed about the beauty of a line of poetry. I have ranted about how irritated I am by the mind-numbing pedantry of shoehorning "transition words" to conceal weak paragraph transitions.

At other times, when I sense that fatigue is setting in for students, I have gotten myself worked up about utter nonsense. I have yelled at kids for playing with their hair, accusing them of mocking my baldness. I have ranted about students saying it is cold when the L.A. temperature dips below 60 degrees, but I have also ranted on behalf of students—and myself—when the classroom becomes unreasonably cold or hot. I have opened the door and screamed into the hallway about it. Kids appreciate that and are often settled by it and motivated to try despite the conditions. If, on the other hand, I catch a student doing their homework for another class during mine, I will launch a jealous rage that another teacher's class matters more than mine.

Mostly I reserve my feigned rage for subject-matter gripes or sometimes even castigate the entire class for some common offense—a cliché left unattended, wordiness run amok. When I am complaining about student deficits, it is never with contempt for the students; my gripe is with us—teachers, schools, whatever has led them astray.

I have found that students appreciate the energy, the passion, and the emotion of these outbursts. They appreciate that I am making the effort to amuse them or excite them, to engage them, to demonstrate overstatement and irony and absurdity.

Not every teacher wishes to veer as far as I do into silliness, but I believe it's useful for any teacher to consider projecting a light-hearted presence of some kind. It is a powerful and good-natured way to show strength and confidence. It can also serve as an antidote to the dreaded common enemy of students and teachers: boredom.

14

Fun Is the Goal, Always

This is how much my students hate the tedium they too often suffer at our hands: though glad to be done with middle school, many of them miss the food fights in the cafeteria, the fight fights in the hallways, and the teacher meltdowns in the classroom.

I doubt they would really wish to return to the violence or volatility, but the complaint underscores just how bored they feel in school much of the time.

To be fair—to us, I mean—our students are at an age that tends to make them easily bored. They experience time slower than we do, and they are naturally restless, stuck, as they are, in the limbo between childhood and adulthood. Ask them how their weekend was. Or their winter or summer break. The typical answer I get is that it was great, plenty of time to sleep, but then it got boring. And they'll admit that though they are always anxious for school to be over, they are also, usually anxious for it to begin again.

They are prisoners of their emotions and sometimes their hormones, and some have yet to develop much, if any, intellectual curiosity. Schools don't make it any easier with all the routines, regimentation, and all the waiting. School activities can mitigate some of the boredom for some students, but most rely on us to make school more tolerable by making our classes as fun as possible.

Students almost always learn more when they are enjoying it. Finding fun ways for them to access the curriculum sometimes

DOI: 10.4324/9781003538936-18

> Students almost always learn more when they are enjoying it.

require extra effort on our part, but that work is generally worth it, and often save us in the long-run.

Getting Students Together

Student collaboration has value for many reasons. It provides students with the experience of working with others, it encourages learning through exploration and discovery, and it helps kids develop their listening skills. And it can be fun for kids or at least help them transcend the tedium—though such outcomes are far from certain.

Group activities need to be high interest and well-structured with accountability baked in. Otherwise, students can end up off-task, socializing or even break down and splinter into classroom friend group conversations. Getting to know the students in my classes has enabled me to better gauge how much managing and monitoring they need to stay focused and on-task.

Kids don't always want to work together. Some are picky about who they will talk to. Others may not want to talk to anyone else in the room. We have to decide how far to force the issue. Encouragement is always preferable to consequence, but there isn't always a choice.

I have sometimes devoted days or even weeks to getting students to work with each other, giving them simple high-interest—and even non-academic—group objectives until they become comfortable with collaboration. Whatever the challenges of student group work, overcoming them is worth the effort.

There is no shortage of literature on the subject of student collaboration—methods of grouping, the assigning of rotating roles within each group to ensure accountability and shared effort, evaluation techniques that can include students grading each other. However much knowledge you gather and advice you get on these techniques, it will work most effectively if your approach also comes from your own sensibilities and that invaluable knowledge you are developing about your students. And, of course, the lessons learned from the successes and failures of actually trying it.

Creating Enjoyment

There has also been a lot written about project/product-based learning, and for good reason. The creative impulse is a powerful one, especially for young people. Making things, especially things of value, can be a source of pride and a very enjoyable way to learn.

As an English teacher, I have always tried to find ways of publishing student work. For years, I taught journalism and helped students produce a weekly school newspaper. I saw their pride at having a byline, watching other students read what they'd written. It made them more willing to work on their writing. I have seen the same effect from publishing student poems and stories in a school literary journal, and, of course, from getting student personal narratives into the pages of local or national newspapers and websites.

Publishing student work in these ways can require a lot of extra time and effort, and that is not always realistic, especially when we are not compensated for those additional hours. The most basic form of publishing student work is, of course, posting it on the walls of the classroom. I like to require students in other classes to do a reading walk around the room and then share their impressions of some of the work. Reading work aloud or other forms of presentation are also effective ways of encouraging students to take pride in their work.

Writing and performing dramatic scenes, writing and producing dramatic films, creating short documentaries are a medium for project-based assignments for any academic subject. Historical reenactments are great as are creative science experiments such as the old favorite rocket building. A nephew of mine built a computer modem in a high school science class back in the 1990s and was still recalling the experience fondly when he was in law school.

The success of such product-based assignments is often made clear by the transforming dynamic of student and teacher.

Rather than having to accost students and ask them questions for understanding (or just asking them what they are doing and when they will start working), we end up getting accosted by students, motivated by their objective, asking the very same questions. When we get good at it—and, sometimes, lucky too—the learning becomes the means to an end, the motivation inherent in that project goal.

Win or Lose

Most of the students I have taught enjoy competing with each other. The desire to win is a strong motivator for a lot of kids and losing a casual academic-based competition in a classroom is not likely to cause them too much anguish; in fact, these are good opportunities for them to learn how to deal with losing.

I discovered just how valuable classroom competitions can be one semester when the principal put virtually the entire basketball team I coached and many of their friends in an elective writing class and the only way I could get them to do anything—other than endlessly clown each other—was to put them in teams and create reading and writing competitions. Pretty soon they were showing up early to class and some were even doing extra homework to prepare for the competitions.

Some easy competitions I have organized are informal and formal debates, mock quiz shows, speed write-offs, research treasure hunts. Mostly these are group activities, but there are also opportunities for individualized competitions, like vocab/spelling bees. Digital devices and educational software have made creating, running, and scoring these activities much easier.

A personal favorite for me are the style, grammar, and usage tests I make up with incentives for anyone who can get a perfect score first with five or ten tries. Some of my questions include references to the students in the class. Many of the questions are, what students refer to as, trolling questions, such as "which one of these is a run-on sentence"—the answer is three words long; the 2156-word sentence is not. Sometimes, I put an intentional mistake in the test, with extra credit for anyone who catches it.

Sometimes competitions can get contentious, which can be exhausting, but satisfying for the high level of engagement it demonstrates.

Culture of Fun

Educating kids is a serious endeavor, which might be the best reason to keep things as light as possible whenever we can.

Some of our students are under enormous pressure—trying to satisfy parental expectations, rescue the family from poverty or trying to emerge out of the shadows of successful parents and/or siblings. They can easily get stuck in the academic quicksand of grades and all the transactionalism that can pound the life out of learning.

Creating a culture and mood emphasizing fun in the classroom can help boost the morale of our students, get kids beyond their stress and focus, at least temporarily, on learning.

> Creating a culture and mood emphasizing fun in the classroom can help boost the morale of our students, get kids beyond their stress and focus, at least temporarily, on learning.

I am not suggesting educators must be entertainers—though it by no means hurts if we are at least a little entertaining at times. And fun doesn't always mean funny—though kids usually appreciate humor. Sometimes just helping students have an emotional experience connected to their learning is meaningful and enjoyable. Helping them relax about some difficult assignment we are asking them to do or some difficult material we are expecting them to absorb—offering them a realistic and optimistic approach—can open them up to learning.

I have found this immensely useful in teaching students to write better. One of the most challenging aspects of writing well is mastering efficiency. So many students— and adults too—get wordy, their prose bloated with overstatement and redundancies. It is really difficult to write efficiently, to maximize meaning and minimize words (perhaps I have demonstrated the problem myself in this book). For students, some of the expressive excessiveness are conditioned. Students get told to write a page or two pages or five. Success gets measured, at least in part, by the square inch. When I show students how overwritten their work is, they can feel overwhelmed. Paralyzed by the fear that if they become efficient writers and cut all the extra words, the meandering nonsense that says essentially nothing, they will have too little, or nothing left on the page. A fun exercise to exorcize the bad habits is to have them intentionally write a page or two of nonsense. Filler. Bullshit. Lean hard in that direction—and see just how ridiculously wordy they can make something. I have found that and other bad writing exercises can be cathartic and enjoyable, and it is fun to read them aloud and laugh at how bad they are.

When students ask for extra credit assignments, usually toward the end of a grading period, I try to come up with something topical and humorous—and sometimes a little sadistic. For example, after Illinois Governor Rod Blagojevich was imprisoned for selling President Obama's senate seat to the highest bidder, I offered extra credit for writing iambic pentameter verse about it—and they had to rhyme with the name Blagojevich at least once. I have also offered extra credit for a variety of wordplay assignments—like writing a sentence using the same word as at least three different parts of speech, like the famous "Buffalo buffalo buffalo buffalo buffalo." (Look up the explanation if you're interested.) I know a math teacher who gives extra credit to anyone who can make a math equation out of the digits of that day's date, like for August 4, 2021: $8 - 4 - 2 + 0 = 2 \times 1$.

Students appreciate anything that breaks the monotony and lightens the mood. I sometimes enjoy making a wall of quotes, posting profound or ridiculous or just random things students say in class with their names beneath them. If I can, I'll describe the hidden brilliance in the statement. It is a celebration of the spoken word and a good way to deal with disruption in a positive way and then move on. Other times I'll write up satirical referrals (those are the forms we are supposed to fill out to report students' misbehavior in our district). Rather than write the actual offense, I'll write something silly, like, "Playing with her hair, mocking my baldness." The student knows what they were actually doing that got my attention and, usually, will stop, appreciating that I made a joke out of it. They save those fake referrals as souvenirs from my class.

Some of our students have little joy in their lives; they need us to model ways to create it out of small things. Some of our students have yet to develop much intellectual curiosity; they need us to model the value of learning things and knowing things. Many of our students find school agonizing; they need to see us having fun and at least trying to help them have fun.

And if kids aren't enjoying our classes, I think we ought to wonder how much they are learning.

15

Plan to Be Spontaneous

Much advice given to new teachers is about planning and organization. Any teacher whoever got to the end of the lesson plan with 20 minutes left of the class understands why.

I learned the hard way to over plan and sometimes over structure my classes. Students still complain on the first and last day of every semester when they realize I've got a real lesson for them. But I have also discovered that my ultimate goal as a teacher goes far beyond structure and regularity and that, at my best, the preparation and structure frees me up to be spontaneous, especially in response to student interest, need, and mood.

It actually reminds me of my brief career in stand-up comedy—and my observations of the more accomplished comic colleagues. I created my set routine, characters, and bits and jokes and got a lot of laughs but didn't really develop the routine much and after a while it got stale. Meanwhile, I watched the success of those comics who were always ready to just riff with the audience and, in a sense, collaborate with them on the comedy, and then find a way into their prepared material. I was young and didn't have the confidence to try that kind of spontaneity. Now, as a teacher, I have that spontaneity, and have found it an effective way to make a class more student-centered.

DOI: 10.4324/9781003538936-19

The Pivot

Being spontaneous supports what I believe ought to be our most important goals for students: depth of learning, enjoyment of the experience, and appreciation of, comfort with, and skill at learning.

Students arrive in our classrooms each day carrying the sometimes heavy baggage of their lives. They aren't always in the mood for us or our lesson. Mostly, the regularity and routines and our confidence in the strength of our teaching and the power of our expectations is what they need to get past their reluctance and transcend their mental and emotional distractedness through the curriculum. But there are times when they need something else.

I remember when a series of murders in the community around our school cast a cloud over the lives of our students. One kid lost a cousin, another had witnessed a killing. Kids were not in the mood for business as usual—nor should they have been. I let students talk and express their trauma and grief, and together we found our way, organically, to poetry about war and violence, and we were able to simultaneously learn and heal—and, perhaps most important, discover the healing power of literature.

Other times I'll read the room and see that kids aren't feeling the lesson. It's just not landing. I can always try to coax them through it, but sometimes I know we are all better off if we work together toward something slightly—or sometimes radically—different.

You may not feel the same comfort about the pivot. Your curriculum may not lend itself to nearly as much spontaneity. As with pretty much everything else about teaching—and learning—one size does not fit all. But an open mind to the spontaneous influence can be highly useful, especially if you work at a school that, like the one where I teach, is prone to sudden crises.

> But an open mind to the spontaneous influence can be highly useful.

Unexpected Opportunities

Emergency assemblies, multiple spur-of-the-moment student summons, unscheduled field trips that snatch half the kids from your class, tech disasters—Wi-Fi outages, computer crashes, district network hacks, or projector bulb blowouts—these are but a few examples of events that can hurl our lesson plans into disarray.

Such disruptions ought not happen—and should certainly not be routine—but for some of us they are a constant challenge. Group work can suddenly fall apart with half the students pulled from a class, student presentations can't happen when three of the six students due to present their projects suddenly, without warning, are meeting with the principal. When the internet goes down, it almost always makes at least something we need for class inaccessible. These can be moments of panic, frustration, and even anger for a teacher. In fact, the more experienced we are at pivoting and improvising, the better prepared we are for the unexpected and when we are prepared for the unexpected, it can be an opportunity for spontaneous invention that can lead to unexpected pique learning moments, not to mention innovations and discoveries that can become part of our teaching repertoire.

In my third or fourth year of teaching, back when our school had no air-conditioning and my decrepit classroom had no windows, we had to endure a particularly hot October and by late morning each day that classroom became uninhabitable. Fans were useless. Propping the door open accomplished little. My classes ended up outside, crowded around crusty benches and tables beneath a small awning, and I had to improvise. I taught them sensory descriptive as we moved from shade to shade, writing about our surroundings. Every year since then, that assignment—going outside and describing the sounds, sights, and smells—has became a regular feature of my class.

In fact, improving itself has become a staple of my teaching.

Riffing in the Classroom

Kids love to derail our teaching objectives. They will, at times, devolve structured group discussion and discovery into gossip and chit-chat and, when we are trying to teach them something through direct instruction, someone will often strive to knock us off-topic. They have their techniques, focusing usually on what they know about us. A kid told me he had an eighth-grade science teacher who loved football … "Monday morning, during NFL season and playoffs, we just got him going and didn't have to do any science."

I used to fight such efforts to derail my learning objective which I understood as a battle of wills the students, deep down, wanted to lose. I still believe that—they want us to make them do the work—but now there are times that I give in and sometimes, just for the fun and the irony of it, I instigate the distraction. I do it because I have come to realize how much students learn in the casual discussions of these interruptions. I believe they are more receptive to learning, more open, because they feel some agency and ownership over what they are doing.

There is, of course, a give and take to this—and I do ultimately have to control how long the digressions last—but they are valid and they are valuable. At my best, I find a way to tie the digression directly to the lesson and sometimes the students create that transition for me, or I can at least make it seem that way.

A few years ago, I began to start some of my classes this way, in a digression. Usually, I would just start talking to the class, asking them questions about things that were going on at school or in the news or I'd overhear a student conversation as I was trying to settle the class and run with it. I appreciated the way it relaxed students and helped them get settled in and get past all the outside distractions in their lives. And then we'd find a way to the lesson—or, sometimes, the digression would take us to a different lesson. That is the luxury of experience, a mental and physical library of material to teach and ways to teach it.

During the distance learning of the pandemic, this method became a staple of my teaching, and since then, it has been a part of my teaching brand—like those standup comics I used to admire when I watched them before and after my set, bantering but finding a way into their routine. I especially appreciate when it seems like a student or students created the assignment. Sometimes, in fact, they have.

Creating a casual atmosphere like this may not be your thing. It doesn't have to be; though, I do believe there can be value for all of us in any method that relaxes students and opens them up to learning—and also recognizes the hard work we should always expect from them.

There are so many external pressures placed on teachers—to go along with our own inner-struggles and self-expectations. Anything we can do to relieve that pressure is essential to us, and to our students.

16

Create Authenticity

High school students are restless. It seems to be part of growing up. They appreciate the value of their time and suspect we are wasting much of it. That is especially true when they get after-school or weekend jobs and begin to get paid by the hour, though unemployed freshmen can be just as suspicious of the actual value of our classes.

At least once a month, I hear students ask why we are learning something—and I know I always must be prepared to answer that question. Just as often, I hear a generalized complaint about school and the uselessness of what they are being taught.

I try to respect such concerns from restless students, help them to understand some of the reasons for how I am asking them to spend all those hours in my class, and they seem to appreciate my efforts to explain and, even more so, my efforts to make their learning as authentic and meaningful as possible.

The worst insult for this current generation of students seems to be some version of, "You're fake." The greatest compliment something on the order of: "That's real" or "He's for real," or, if a teacher ever earns it, "You're the realist teacher I have." This should tell us something—not just about our interactions with the kids we teach but about what we ask them to learn and what we do to help make it meaningful.

Flipping the Transactional

It is not easy to get students to forget, even for a moment, that they are students forced to be with us and that we are judging them with the power of a grade.

They may sometimes seem comfortable with their oppression—enough to make us use our authority to address their behavior and challenge their attitude. It is just one of the many self-contradictions of their condition. They demonstrate dependency while almost certainly wishing us to help them become more responsible and give them just enough space to grow.

One way I have found to promote this project is by creating opportunities for student self-assessment. It is not a matter of transferring the grading process over to them. They want and need external accountability and, if we are fair and encouraging, value our input. But whenever possible, require them to critique their own performance. Not just a number or a grade but with a written explanation. I also like to give them permission to critique my assignments before, during, or after they've attempted them.

Not every student may be ready for that responsibility, but it is a low-risk proposition; at worst, some students won't take the offer seriously, and even that can be the beginning of a conversation about our teaching and their learning and how both might improve.

Self-reflection can help to pull students out of their passivity. Almost any midterm or final I create requires students to reflect on what they have done in the class and what they have learned and how they might have done more. Some students will give an answer they believe will make me grade them more favorably—usually some perfunctory version of "I worked hard but I know I could have worked harder," but even insincerity pushes kids cumulatively toward the influence of their truth. That echo of *I can do better*

> Self-reflection can help to pull students out of their passivity.

can eventually become a motivational mantra. I also, usually, ask students to evaluate me and the class. Again, an opportunity for sycophancy, but also an opportunity, if I have truly earned their trust, to offer blunt criticism of my teaching—another way for us to keep it real.

I try to promote the flexibility to meet students somewhere other than the docility and compliance that school so often demands. Sometimes that means an alternate assignment, something negotiated with a student to help them learn and demonstrate the essential skills and knowledge. This is not always possible, but when it is, the compromise offers a kind of personalization and ownership that can overcome a lot of student resistance. Sometimes it is the assessment we can modify and personalize. Sometimes we can offer a variety of ways to demonstrate learning or mastery and it costs us nothing to indulge students in negotiating their own assessment. A lot of kids don't want to bother—it is actually a challenging task—and many just aren't yet comfortable with that kind of autonomy—though merely introducing the idea of it can get them thinking and moving toward being more self-directed learners.

The same can be true of letting students create some of their assignments—or even requiring them to create at least part of one, for each other or for themselves. It is a way of giving them a bigger stake in their learning and another way to get them thinking about their responsibility for their own education.

I have done this in formal ways—assigning them to create questions for a reading or prompts for an essay—and I have done it by taking things students wrote or said in class and made them into parts of a future assignment for their class.

This happens a lot when I teach film study. Students want me to show and analyze their favorite films. I will usually agree but only if they write up some study questions and writing prompts for the film. A lot of students will disdain the offer but those willing to do the work say that creating an assignment teaches them a lot about analyzing drama, character, cinematic techniques, and so on.

> Any time we can offer students choices about their learning, we are offering them a deeper degree of participation and a real sense of recognition and respect.

Any time we can offer students choices about their learning, we are offering them a deeper degree of participation and a real sense of recognition and respect. It is not an all-or-nothing proposition. Almost nothing we do as teachers ever is.

Make the Argument

Whenever we ask students to spend time and effort on something, we are making an implicit assertion that it will, in some way, benefit them—hopefully, a chance to acquire essential skills and knowledge.

We should assume that every student has a voice in their head making the counter-argument—that we are wasting their time with BS—so it is not a bad idea, at least some of the time, to clearly articulate the specific benefits available to them through the assignment, whether or not they ask us to.

I do not necessarily mean we need to pitch the academic task at their potential skepticism. I actually prefer embedding the rationale in the text of the assignment—as a footnote somewhere or, better still, baked into the description of the task.

This does not promise to prevent the gripes and groans of students who just don't want to expend mental energy. Nor does it, by any stretch, assure that every student will enthusiastically take on the assignment. It is part of a message of collaboration and inclusion for students. It is part of the long and sometimes tedious process of coaxing students out of apathy and passivity and helping them take ownership of their own learning.

An Authenticity Mindset

Promoting authenticity for our students is an endless and often slow process. Many come to us with quite the opposite attitude toward their education, and there is a good chance they are spending much of their school day still in that oppressive and transactional space. That is perhaps the most compelling reason why we should do what we can to offer them something real.

It starts with our own perspective about our teaching. Think beyond the walls of the school. How can we continually connect our students to the world in which they need to somehow find their place? It doesn't mean constantly reminding them of their impending adulthood. There is no need; they already know. Nor does it mean we can't help them sometimes forget that childhood is slipping away—if we are making the learning fun, then we are helping them make adolescence the oasis it can and ought to be.

Keeping it real for our students means remembering that it is our privilege to be trusted with the minds of other people's children. It means seeing the best in those kids, even when—especially when—they are at their worst. It means listening to them with our hearts as well as our minds.

It means being honest with the kids and with ourselves, and having the humility to recognize our limitations, in the moment, to make the effort to overcome them and maybe inspire the students to overcome theirs.

That is quite likely the realist thing we can do for them.

17

Manageable Differentiation

Despite the sadly persistent segregation throughout much of our education system—and the society it reflects—every class we will ever teach is a study in diversity. It may not superficially appear that way, but superficial assumptions and assessments are not very useful for us.

Over more than three decades I have taught only four students who identified as "white" and about the same number who identified as "Asian-American," but my students represent a rich tapestry of cultures and family histories with roots throughout the United States, Mexico and Central America, the Caribbean and the African continent. Some are only children, others come from medium-size and large families. Some students live with both parents, others have single parents or foster parents or are being raised by grandparents or other relatives. Some reside in group homes. Others and their families are unhoused or are housing insecure. And so on. I do not know all such details about all my students, but I am always cognizant that they bring to our class different experiences and challenges as well as a variety of talents, perspectives, attitudes, and ambitions.

Some of our students may have learning challenges identified in an Individual Education Plans; others may have undiagnosed ones just as formidable. Some of our students are still learning English as their second language. All students have unique ways that they think, express themselves, and learn. Thinking about ourselves and all the nuanced ways that we acquire knowledge and remember things and problem solve, we can begin to imagine all the different learning styles of the kids in our classrooms.

How we respond to those differences can have a significant influence on our success as teachers.

The Impossible

Teachers, especially when we are new, are often told to "differentiate instruction" or asked how we differentiate without clear or realistic directions, and we are sometimes given the impression that we are supposed to design a specific curriculum and delivery of instruction for every student.

That might be a reasonable ideal. If we were given the resources—small enough classes, adequate time to do that kind of massive preparation, and perhaps a teacher's assistant or two, but what many teachers are given instead are unrealistic directives and subtle shaming.

None of us should ever accept that nonsense. If we care about our students and make the effort to know as much as we can about them, we can take realistic steps, with a clear conscience, to do the best we reasonably can for all the learners in our classroom.

Variation in Pedagogy

Unless we have very small classes, we cannot realistically modify every lesson to meet the specific learning needs of every student. Adapting and reasonably stretching themselves cognitively should be a natural part of student learning.

One way to achieve maximum accessibility is to vary our teaching approaches with a mix of direct instruction, class discussion and inquiry, group work, projects, games, traditional and imaginative assessments, and so on. Every learning approach plays differently to the comforts and discomforts of each student, providing them a variety of contexts in which to shine or grow.

Such variation also keeps our classes interesting and engaging.

Modest Modification

There are many modifications with which we can reasonably target the learning needs of specific students. I will describe some that have worked for me. They are just a start and often the most practical and effective modifications come from knowledge of our students, expertise in our subject and a deepening understanding of how our students learn.

Scaffolding Vocabulary

Scaffolding vocabulary is a common and fairly easy differentiation. Anyone who has taught second language learners knows how essential it is to provide new vocabulary prior to any reading—and probably also knows how useful it is for many native English speakers to see and define unfamiliar words before reading a passage or as part of a comprehension check every few paragraphs. Sometimes, I provide the definitions. Other times, I ask students to look the words up and sometimes demonstrate that they can use them accurately in sentences. When I do that, I often award extra credit to kids who can use multiple new words in a single sentence.

Extra Time

Allowing students the time they need to complete assignments is an accommodation required by a lot of student IEPs. Such a mandate is easy for psychologists, counselors, and administrators to scribble or type into a form, it can be quite a bit more challenging for a classroom teacher to implement.

Giving extra time to some students can complicate the pacing of our class. Meanwhile, every time a student returns from an absence—or from a meeting with the counselor during the first half of our class—we have to figure out how to get them caught up. Frustration is pointless. Flexibility is essential. In that sense, we ought not be thrown too far off at having to differentiate the time allotted to each student to complete an assignment. We ought to get used to students working at different paces and find ways to ensure that those who work fast can keep learning and that

> We ought to get used to students working at different paces and find ways to ensure that those who work fast can keep learning and that those who need more time don't fall behind.

those who need more time don't fall behind. Experience can increase our comfort level in calibrating all that variation—and with experience we should have an extensive inventory of materials that can help us keep fast-finishing students engaged and learning while their peers get the extra time they need.

Alternatives

Differentiating instruction is always a challenge, and we have to manage our expectations and the sometimes unrealistic demands of others.

Our students have different reading levels and some of them struggle and can get demoralized with reading material to which other students should be exposed. Those texts can be modified to a more accessible using software that should be available to any teacher expected to provide such accommodations. Of course, handing out a modified text to one or more students complicates instruction. It complicates reading aloud and may limit our options to small group reading—if there are enough students reading the modified text—or else sustained silent reading.

Not a bad idea to mix it up anyway—vary our in-class reading strategies. We can have whole class read around and discussion, and our scaffolding, in real time, can sometimes eliminate the need for textual modifications, helping all students access deeper levels of understanding, make connections, and appreciate the beauty and value of great literature and compelling argument

We can also experiment with offering alternative texts and assignments to struggling learners—or reading choices for everyone. This can be cumbersome but experience and an inventory of assignments we've hopefully accumulated, can make such flexibility increasingly more comfortable. Showing students a willingness to be flexible for the sake of their learning is a powerful statement and can inspire a deeper level of trust and motivation.

Grouping for Differentiation

It is worth noting that group discussion and group work lend themselves well to differentiation. Always important to group students with thoughtful intention and figure out, sometimes by trial and error, to whom your struggling learners respond best, and which students feel most comfortable in a leadership role.

It doesn't always work. At least not without some intervention on our part. Some students can be difficult to collaborate with; I have had students complain and request group changes. These are opportunities for students to understand the consequences of their conduct, and sometimes helping students understand the power of patience and compromise. Peer pressure is a powerful force—one we can leverage for student growth.

Differentiated Grading

Most of us come to teaching with at least some preconceived ideas about grades. Mostly these are a mixture of our experiences as students and our general sensibilities about fairness and value.

We may find ourselves at a school offering a lot of guidance about grading policies, or we may find ourselves making it up as we go along. Most of us are pretty quick to understand the immense responsibility of issuing grades, especially in high school, particularly to ambitious students wishing to attend competitive colleges. If we are struggling with student discipline, we may start to reach for our grading authority as our greatest—and perhaps only—power. Hopefully, we will quickly get over that misconception. We should also be quick to discover how ambiguous and complicated grades are, and how little they sometimes have to do with the objectives of our classes.

> Rigidity and consistency may seem the fair and responsible approach but not when cold objectivity become heartless neglect of the needs of students, and not if we forget that our priority as educators—without exception—should be to maximize student learning.

Rigidity and consistency may seem the fair and responsible approach but not when cold objectivity become heartless neglect of the needs of students, and not if we forget that our priority as educators—without exception—should be to maximize student learning. Accountability is part of that objective and sometimes students need the hard lessons of disappointment that match insufficient effort. But when the best efforts of struggling learners are insufficient, we can just as easily demoralize them with the heartless calculations of blind objectivity.

Colleges may want our grades to reflect student ability for the sake of their admissions criteria, but we do not work for them. Counselors and admins may want us to prioritize elevating grade averages and graduation rates, but we should never be answerable to such political calculations. We work for our students and grades can be a motivator. When we know our students we can measure kids not against each other but against their potential and their barriers; we can use those grave measurements to help students reinvent themselves and carve their own individual path to success.

Innovation Differentiation

The best differentiations and interventions are often the ones we create based on knowledge and understanding of our students and their unique needs and challenges.

Like figuring out how to help students who struggle to stay in their seats by finding constructive ways to get them up and active. Or turning disruptive students into class leaders by giving them roles and responsibilities.

I have allowed reluctant writers to demonstrate their knowledge by producing a podcast, then submitting a transcript of it with commentary—and I watched them realize that they'd actually written more and gone deeper in their analysis with that assignment than any essay they'd ever struggled with. I have allowed reluctant writers to free-write, to rant about their apprehensions, to get words down and begin to discover their literary or rhetorical voice.

I have encouraged and rewarded students for writing about the emotional distress that is undermining their academic performance and doing relevant research—merging academic skills with their urgent need for emotional comfort. I have also learned by listening to and observing the methods students have figured out on their own for meeting their biggest learning challenges.

I have also learned from colleagues who have discovered their own methods for reaching individual students, elevating their comfort level about accessing the curriculum and sometimes altering their outlook on learning and their image of themselves as students.

Read the Room

Whatever accommodations and differentiations we are compelled to provide, and however we manage to reasonably provide them, we are wise to keep an open mind and a close eye on our students. Observe the joys of their breakthroughs and the frustrations of their struggles and respond positively to both.

When we see students squinting at the whiteboard or the projection screen or the paper in front of them, inquire and investigate and, if they need it, print and project things larger for them—and follow up with parents and the nurse about possible vision problems (or get them to wear the unfashionable glasses they no longer wish to wear or urge them—or help them—replace the broken pair they can no longer use).

Don't rely exclusively on IEPs to tell us students need accommodations. Help them all as best we can. What I am suggesting may sound like adding to the already cumbersome burdens of teaching, but in the long run it can prove to be a shortcut.

We aren't just helping students learn the subject we are teaching. We are helping them learn how to find strategies for their own intellectual growth and academic survival and helping them learn compassion and understanding.

18
Success Is the Means and the End

Student motivation is never a given. Distraction, disinterest, and discouragement perpetually lurk around our classrooms and can sometimes overwhelm our efforts. There is always plenty of blame to cast. *The students just don't care. Their parents don't value education enough. Smartphones are destroying their minds. American culture is anti-intellectual. The administration, the school district, and the whole system doesn't really support student learning. Etc. etc.*

We may be justified in thinking at least some of those things, but diagnosing the problem may not direct us toward a solution. Often, our most reliable motivator is tapping into every child's inherent need for validation and the academic success that, even in small doses, can be a powerful source of that validation.

Understanding the Need

Think of the thrill children feel when they stand on their legs and take their first steps or speak their first coherent phrase or even grow a tooth or another inch. Consider the praise adults give them for these accomplishments.

Now, consider what so many teenagers—particularly the ones challenging us the most in our classes—are hearing from the adults in their lives. Mostly about what they are doing wrong and how annoying they are. Even those kids lucky enough to have parents willing and able to offer positive reinforcement, are no longer nourished to quite the same extent as they once were by the praise of their parents. They need it from other adults—validation that they are more than the object of parental love.

Kids are profoundly sensitive to the ways in which we respond to them. By high school, some have formed negative identities in the image of how they believe they've been perceived. They see themselves as trouble-makers, bad kids, stupid, lazy, and so on. There is a good chance they will assume you or I will also perceive them that way. Convincing them otherwise can be challenging—they usually don't trust it, not at first—but it can be life-changing.

Understanding the Power

I experienced this myself in fifth grade when a teacher made a big fuss about something I had written. It was a description of the street I lived on in New York City, and I really got into it, exaggerating the chaos and noise and I even described the sound of gunfire I'd heard a few months earlier when corrupt NYPD officers had apparently shot a fellow officer in front of my building. My teacher read it to the class and went on about how good it was and then sent it to a friend of hers who published a small literary journal. I had never before thought of myself as smart and had often thought I was stupid. I became a much better student in her class after that, and though it didn't quite last into the next year, I never forgot her belief in me and I think it was part of what eventually led me to believe in myself.

I have seen similar transformations happen with students. A girl I'll call W, on the first day of class, wrote a diatribe about injustice. It was intensely angry and that made it stand out from all the other student responses about how they viewed the state of their world. I told W that she had impressed me and added, "I guess I'm not the first teacher to say that you write really well."

Actually, as it turned out, I was, and it seemed that was all she needed. She became an outspoken leader in the class and a scholar. I found out that the previous year she had been a marginal student. I found out she had a somewhat troubled family life—and plenty of reason for her anger, which softened as she became increasingly successful, not just in English but in all her classes.

That spring, I came across a photocopy I'd made of that paragraph she'd written her first day in my class. It shocked me because in so many ways it wasn't very well written. I hadn't meant to deceive her. I'd felt the anger and intensity and passion in her writing and that still impressed me, but I'd overlooked everything wrong with it—and it was a good thing. Since then, she had actually become a pretty damn good writer and a really good student—and taught me one of the most profound lessons about our positive influence as teachers. That summer, she got an internship with the Los Angeles Times and got a byline in the Metro section of the paper. By her senior year, she was one of our top students and got a scholarship to Pitzer College.

That lesson got reinforced a few years later with a student I'll call J. He had pretty severe learning disabilities. One of the nicest kids I'd ever taught but couldn't write a coherent sentence and could barely speak in a way anyone could understand. But he loved to learn or try to learn. You could see that spark of interest in everything. He was in my journalism class and would try to write articles for the school paper, but none of them were readable. I sat down with him and tried to get at what he was trying to say and show him how to make sense, but I got the feeling my version didn't really express his ideas. He asked if he could write poems and, though poetry is not the usual copy for a newspaper, I agreed. What he wrote was as mystifying as his prose, but obtuse poetry can be brilliant, and I told him he had an original style and that his imagery was powerful and I watched him beam with pride. He produced one or two of these poems a week and really labored over them and used the byline "Poem Man," and after a while I noticed that his poems started to become less obtuse. So did the rest of his writing.

One day that same year, a field trip emptied most of my class and left me only seven students, all of them ineligible for extracurricular activities because their grades were so low, and I watched them come alive and become engaged and enthusiastic when they suddenly believed they were the best students in the room. Every year that I have taught summer school, I encounter students with no academic ambition who seem to be waiting for the right time to drop out of school, but if I can get them to try on at least one assignment and tell them something good about what they have done—even just a sentence or two or an insight or two that really shine—there is a chance they can start to believe in themselves as students.

There is no magic—no all-encompassing shortcut (at least not one that I know of)—to creating opportunities for student success. Mostly, for me, it is awareness combined with a lot of trial and error and from that stumbling, I've discovered a few things.

The Image of Success

> What is a reasonably achievable demonstration of skill or knowledge for each kid?

A good start for me is always to imagine what success could look like for my students. What is a reasonably achievable demonstration of skill or knowledge for each kid? They may all have different strengths, but they all have at least one that can make them shine and, like J, a few moments of success can inspire much more success.

About ten years ago, I started putting student quotes on the wall. These were things that kids said during discussions or sometimes in the heat of an argument or even, sometimes, an offhand thing said upon entering the room. Some were silly in an original way, others were slangy and sometimes bizarre, others were intentionally or unintentionally ironic, others really were quite brilliant, but what mattered was that their words were being immortalized (at least symbolically) with their names below their words. It meant a lot to a lot of them and gave them (and everyone else) a sense of the importance of language and self-expression and a sense of their own importance as thinkers and speakers and writers. What I love about displaying student quotes is that the praise and validation comes simply and powerfully through the action of printing their words in 36 font size and tacking them to the wall.

Creating Ethos

Needless to say, it is not a given that students who have never had success and may not even believe it is possible for them will value the success we make available to them. It has to feel real and we have to seem credible as validators.

Our kids ought to already know we want them to feel good about themselves and achieve in our classes. We ought to assume they are at least a little skeptical of our positive appraisals of them. We don't want to offer them success that doesn't feel sufficiently earned.

It helps if we believe in the success, however small, we are creating for them. I often try to tell students—and remind myself—what I was like at their age, what my intellectual and academic capacities were. I have high expectations for students and hope they have high expectations for themselves, but high generalized expectations should always be tempered with more modest and realistic expectations in the moment.

For me, the most powerful evidence of my sincerity has always come from my expertise in the subject I am teaching. I am confident in what I know about reading for depth and subtlety and what I know about writing and the writing process, and students don't doubt my expertise—especially because I am not afraid to admit what I don't know or aren't sure of. So, even when a kid doubts that a passage they wrote is as good as I say it is, if I stand my ground, and if I believe what I am saying, they will usually come to believe me.

A Context for Everyone's Success

The path to pervasive student success is often paved with authentic teaching that is interactive and developed from our knowledge and fondness for students. It is far easier to create it if we avoid focusing our teaching on knowing things and satisfying some preconceived idea of what is correct.

Focus instead on insight, discovery, articulation, and progress. Value student curiosity, original thought, and an effort to get at and articulate those things. Find ways to measure student progress that advantages students. Vary the means of assessment to give every student a chance to shine. Never stop believing that every student has a reasonable and realistic path to success in our class.

> Value original thought, insight, a strong voice in student writing and speaking, and the effort to get at those things.

And believe in ourselves—in our ability to identify achievement and growth, however incremental, in our students. Be patient with them and teach them patience with themselves.

19

Noise

The first time I stepped into a high school classroom as a teacher, I thought I might be knocked over by that cacophony. The squeaking of metal chair legs, stomping of feet against linoleum tiles, shrieking voices and laughter jolting the air, louder and louder until I thought it all might shatter the windows or blow some fiberglass tiles out of the ceiling.

It set my nerves on edge and made me wonder if I could do this teaching thing.

I have been in a lot of classrooms since that time and am now accustomed to the sound and I am actually quite comfortable with it. I have seen teachers try to yell over that cacophony. I have seen teachers scream for quiet. I have heard myself make those mistakes. I have heard a classroom din swell to a roar. I've seen teachers try to snuff the din before it became a roar because they were afraid they'd never be able to contain it. I have acted on that same fear myself.

The slow growth of my own confidence has helped me get comfortable with the constructive noise of student collaboration and enabled me to trust that my students and I can control it.

Noisy as students can be, they can also be really quiet.

Both conditions can be essential to learning. They can also be impediments.

The Loud Classroom

Classrooms can buzz with student engagement. They thump with student chaos meandering through an unstructured void.

Most experienced teachers can tell almost immediately tell the difference. My own inner detector got activated one morning when a class discussion turned into an argument. We were reading *Fences* and the girls were upset at the revelation that Troy had cheated on Rose. Some of the boys in the class defended him and things nearly got out of hand, but soon I realized that every student in the room was really into this literary dispute. Even the usually quiet kids, those I could hardly ever get to speak. Amid the racket, they felt free to express themselves to the kids around them.

It was an important revelation for me. That we want students talking to each other—we want them learning from each other. We want them to learn how to exchange ideas and listen to one another, argue respectfully, and hold each other intellectually accountable. Perhaps these are lofty goals—and we owe it to kids to believe in them.

It is hard work—for us and our students. It requires us to create just enough structure to encourage accountability and give them tasks that are difficult enough to encourage collaboration, engaging enough to distract them from their distractions, and manageable enough that they aren't tempted by their doubts.

Yet more reasons to know as much as we can about our students. To know what matters to them. What will spark them to work together and listen and be productive. To know which combinations of students are most likely to achieve this result. The trial and error of this teaches us more about our kids and it prepares us for every cohort of kids that will come after. It still gives me great joy when a reading or a discussion sends the kids into mass conflict. The joy gets even sweeter when I pass students in the hallway or on the stairs between classes and hear them still arguing about it. Or when I see that students I have grouped together for academic reasons have become friends.

Sometimes You Just Have to Modulate the Noise Level

Sometimes, even productive student talk can build to headache level, and we might, for our own sanity and to maintain the learning environment, need to bring things down a few decibels.

Calm music can sometimes modulate student voices, though sometimes it just serves to increase the volume of student talk. Sometimes, we have to interject. Get students' attention with a comment or a question or a reminder of some kind. Even if it is mostly a pretext to silence students momentarily and attempt a reset of the noise level.

Stepping into the cacophony to get quiet—to clarify directions, transition to a new activity, or sometimes just to start the class—is an acquired skill for most of us. Experienced teachers have our methods for getting students to stop talking and pay attention. Some train students to respond when they see the teacher's raised hand or some other object held high. I have seen others snap their fingers and get students to join along until enough students are snapping to be noticed by everyone else. Other teachers count to three or count down from three or some other number or have some familiar call and response, like, "One, two, three, eyes on me," and the students respond with, "One, two, eyes on you." A gimmick that might not work for every high school cohort, but some teachers can pull it off.

As a new teacher I was told not to raise my voice to get quiet and I quickly discovered why. No one likes being yelled at and my students were more likely to ignore my raised voice than my regular voice, but sometimes I had to do something to get their attention. In a desperate moment, I yelled at a kid about something innocuous—had I given him the assignment he'd missed when he was absent—and for half a second all the students turned at the sound of me yelling at him, and then I had their attention and managed to get everyone to listen to me.

I have used that trick ever since. Get their attention somehow—whatever works—and then calmly say what needs to be said. With experience and reputation, these tricks are less necessary but with experience, also, I have become more patient.

I can now stand before a noisy and distracted group of students and calmly, politely ask them for their attention until I get it, with confidence that eventually I will.

One of my favorite lines—inspired by the end of a Kurt Vonnegut speech—is the ironic, "Can I please have your sweetly faked attention?" (Vonnegut's actual line is "I thank you for your sweetly faked attention.") Kids kind of love the ironic permission to only fake paying attention to me—which many of them probably do, at times, without permission, though when I say this they actually, perhaps self-consciously, do seem to listen.

Another ironic approach is to stand before the class and whisper. It doesn't always work, but sometimes, if enough kids somehow notice I am whispering, they become curious and quiet down to listen.

The advice I most often give new and struggling teachers is: try not to get frustrated with the chaos or the noise, especially when students ignore or otherwise resist your attempts to restore order. Losing your cool only alienates students, especially those who aren't part of the problem, and it erodes student confidence in you. Having said that, it is entirely understandable to lose one's cool under such circumstances. We are human and things can sometimes feel unmanageable and overwhelming. I've been there. I've lost it and then regained my dignity and moved on and the kids are usually willing to forgive. Surprising as it may sometimes seem, they really want us to succeed.

If possible, avoid name-checking students to get them quiet. When you do have to admonish students—by name or otherwise, for any reason—try to keep it upbeat. Exude positivity as much as possible. Students appreciate it, especially those who cannot seem to help but exude negativity all the time.

As soon as you can get students on your side, all of this gets much easier.

Mostly, I have found, when a classroom is well-structured and kids feel productive and successful, it gets easy to keep kids on-task, most of the time, and get their attention when we need to.

The Quiet Classroom

> Educators have come to understand that silence does not always equal learning.

When I began teaching, quiet was often a measure of a teacher's effectiveness. Not so much anymore. Educators have come to understand that silence does not always equal learning.

Quiet can result from lethargy and boredom, from confusion and anxiety. Sleeping or half-asleep students tend to be quiet. So are students zoned out on video games or the endless digital scrolls of their phones or just chilling to the music piping through their earbuds. Quiet also happens when students won't collaborate or even talk to each other.

A quiet classroom, in and of itself, is not a meaningful goal and I, for one, have had to disabuse myself of that notion. I still sometimes have to remind myself that student talk can be a desired outcome.

That said, quiet is a sometimes-necessary condition for intellectual growth and academic success. Challenging texts require deep concentration. So do complex calculations and meaningful writing assignments. That level of focus can only really be achieved in something at least resembling silence. Students who say they write better while listening to music—particularly vocal music—or streaming a show or multitasking a video game or the multiplicity of group chats are deluding themselves. The quality of the work they produce under such conditions will almost certainly prove as much.

> Many of our students have not yet developed the mental muscles necessary for deep concentration and focus.

Many of our students have not yet developed the mental muscles necessary for deep concentration and focus. Their lives, in and out of school, may be noisy and chaotic. They may not have a place where they are ever alone and free of distraction. When asked to read or write in silence, some will complain. They will say that they are bored. They are right, and it is precisely because they have not yet developed the ability for deep and complex academic thinking. They have built up no endurance for reading or writing.

It is on us to provide them with opportunities to gain those essential abilities, whether they think they want them or not.

We should be willing to start with small and manageable goals. Five minutes of silent reading. Then seven. Then ten. Quietly composing a paragraph and then, perhaps after peer and teacher feedback, quietly revising it into something effective and engaging. Small steps—keeping in mind that we are not just helping them learn academic skills and knowledge but also develop academic habits and strengths.

The Right Balance

Every cohort of students presents its own unique opportunities and challenges. Experienced teachers understand this and use their knowledge and understanding of their students in finding ways to make their class fun and meaningful. We also understand that our needs matter too and should be a factor in how we calculate the noise formula for our classes.

Some kids can only do quiet work in small bursts and need to build up their endurance; others may only be able to do small group work for short stretches before they lose focus, veer off task, and lurch across appropriate behavioral boundaries. Alternating silent work with group talk and collaboration can maximize learning opportunities and provide opportunities for student growth. It can also help us keep our piece of mind amid the sometimes-deafening roar of thirty or forty student voices.

Transitioning from talk to quiet and back to talk is sometimes smooth and sometimes not. Remain determined and generally insistent. Some students will keep talking when they should be reading or writing. Do not capitulate to their recalcitrance. Don't lose your cool, either. Be encouraging. They might be resisting out of insecurity about being able to do the assignment. Let them know you believe in their ability and that you will help them succeed.

And don't become the noise in the room. I have watched novice teachers tell students to start reading or writing and then keep talking—reiterating directions or whatever. If a student raises their hand, approach them and answer their question in a whisper—unless the student has brought up something everyone else needs to hear about. Show reverence for the silence that is required for academic progress and students will come to respect it.

When it is time for student discussion and collaboration, show the same reverence for it. Let students know how important it is for them to learn teamwork and the necessary compromises. Some students may be reluctant to talk to each other and you may find them sitting together in silence. You might find the three or four students you've assigned to work together staring at the floor or their phones like people waiting for their number to come up at the DMV.

That is an indicator that you probably need to create a classroom culture of familiarity and friendliness in order for kids to collaborate. Sometimes that means giving students fun—only marginally academic—tasks in order for them to get comfortable talking to each other and working together. Like the spaghetti tower marshmallow challenge. It may take a while—weeks, sometimes—to achieve that comfort level for students. This was the case for a lot of teachers and students returning from the Covid-19 distance learning and has remained a challenge as we continue to teach kids impacted by the isolation of those many months. However long it takes to help them become effective at peer collaboration, it will be time well spent on the students' behalf.

It is an equally valuable investment of time to help students develop an ability to read or write quietly for a sustained period.

A student's ability to successfully collaborate with peers and their ability to achieve deep concentration in their individual work are as important to their future success as any academic knowledge or skill we hope they will learn.

20
What They Call Classroom Management

I still have nightmares that go something like this:

I am in a classroom full of students and none of them will listen to me. Some seem not to know I am there despite my attempts to get their attention. Others sneer and stare and disregard me. Objects are flying across the room. Kids are sitting on a window ledge. My desk is being ransacked. Finally, one student speaks to me and says, "Why don't you do something? What kind of teacher are you?" And so on.

I remember learning that term "classroom management" and thinking it sounded so benign and that it ought to be called something more like, "Wrestling the souls of three dozen teenagers in all their angst and agitation."

I have had my battles. The worst days were as a day-to-day substitute teacher, and I quickly recognized that things were much easier when the teacher I was subbing for was well-organized and had left clear instructions and held students accountable even when they were not there. The worst days were replacing teachers who had been gone a long time, leaving kids educationally neglected. On my most demoralizing day, I was left with students whose teacher had fallen ill in that very classroom several weeks before, and no one knew if he would ever return. Those kids were rebelling against the depraved indifference of the world—and for that day I was collateral damage.

By the time I had a full-time teaching position and was in charge of two-hundred students in seven classes, I understood that student behavior was not so much something to manage as it was a reflection of student/teacher rapport, student engagement with the class, along with how students were handling their emotional lives and how the teacher was responding to signs of their distress.

I also discovered that whenever I was thinking of students as a management challenge, I was probably faltering.

Student behavior can be one of the most stressful aspects of teaching and when things get bad, it can be misery. We are outnumbered. By a lot. Kids are not always great at rising above their own angst and misery. They are restless and tend to be emotionally volatile. The pressures in their lives are mounting, and some fear they have already failed in some important way. All of them are all prone to massive self-doubt. Adulthood stalks them like a rogue bear, threatening to pounce. And they wish we would fix it all for them. If you've ever been in a relationship with someone who expected far more from you than was humanly possible, that was part of your teacher training.

When we are new to the classroom, our students are not; they know more about tormenting teachers than we know about protecting, deflecting, and redirecting. Arriving with a thick skin helps, but many of us may have to add a few more layers.

When we are new, our students, especially those in the upper grades, may regard us—and treat us—like stepparents. It takes time and work to earn trust and respect. Meanwhile, we have to be patient with students and ourselves—and not assume or expect that they will have any patience with us.

Beyond that are some mindsets and techniques that can be useful survival tools. These were—and sometimes still are—mine:

It's (Usually) Not that Serious

It is a little paradoxical. Few jobs are more serious than educating the next generation. But if we approach the mission with too much of that grave seriousness, we will almost certainly annoy and alienate our students and vex ourselves into burnout.

> Teaching is far more manageable with a light heart.

Teaching is far more manageable with a light heart.

Kids know they have to grow up, and they have a good idea how difficult and sometimes painful that task can be. Our academic intentions are a big part of it, and if we can deliver that burden with joy and a little humor, if we can relax and give them permission to relax, most teenagers will ultimately buy-in quickly, work harder, and learn more than if our class is just another tentacle of this monstrous adult world with which we keep threatening them.

When kids act silly or irrational or grouchy, they are grasping at everything they fear they are forever losing from whatever childhood they've been able to sustain. If we show some appreciation for what is left of the child they are compelled to leave behind, then they will more easily start to move past it.

I don't mean we have to complement their displays of immaturity. Just not be all severe about them. Play along for a few seconds, or make a joke or use irony. When kids are clowning around with each other instead of collaborating or discussing, I tell them with exaggerated outrage that fun isn't allowed in class. Somehow the ironic tone—which says to them that I understand and that I am actually glad they are having fun but that I wish they would get back on task—actually gets them to stop.

Kids sometimes do outrageous things in our classrooms. Either forgetting themselves in the moment or deliberately trying to get a reaction from us or their peers. A short list of what comes to memory: squirting hand lotion all over a desk and the floor and each other, suddenly braiding a friend's hair in the middle of class, hiding my water bottle from me, lying on the floor, standing on the desk.

Unless what a student is doing endangers themselves or someone else, I still try to keep it light. "Late night?" "Nap time?" "Are you masticating in class?" (To someone eating), "Are you farding in class?" (To someone applying makeup). Any attempted humor, however lame, is an unexpected expression of forgiveness. Play along. Not too encouraging. Just take the judgment out of their harmless spasms of regression. We are often told not to reward kids for their attempts at attention, but for me, what works better is to give them a few seconds of validation in the spotlight—a kind of unconditional acceptance of who they are at the moment—then get on with class.

For me, those are displays of strength as a teacher, and they are teachable moments—few lessons are more important for them than learning patience and understanding.

However I choose to respond to their goofiness, I try to convey this message, subtextually or otherwise: *you are great, you're going to be great, I understand your resistance to growing up and am confident that you ultimately will.*

This has all become easier since I began to meet some of the most childish students ten years later all grown up, working middle-class adults, mothers and fathers, carrying all the burdens that go along with success. A reminder to me that the kids in my classes every day will likely (hopefully) have a very long time to be adults and carry those burdens. No wonder they might want to postpone it, even just for a few minutes on a Tuesday afternoon.

Give Them the Punchline

Much as I like to get laughs and flex my mediocre comic talents, what I have come to desire even more is to give kids the space to be the funny ones—provided, of course, that it is not too much at the expense of another student. Even if I have to curtail someone's shtick, I always try to give them a few moments in the spotlight.

When there is banter between a student or students and me, I try to set a kid up to get the laugh and have gotten better at that over time. I am comfortable with students ridiculing me—for my bald head, my age, my hearing loss, having so many tabs open on the computer I am projecting on the classroom screen, or whatever else. I might pretend to be offended and even fire back, but always with a playful tone. Again, I find a little of this goes a long way and actually minimizes disruption by reducing conflict.

> Find the give-and-take with students, compromise that elevates and encourages students in small ways and helps maintain a climate that is fun and friendly and earns student cooperation and even compliance in the moments when we might need it.

I encourage you to find ways to lean on your own teaching style toward humor and away from conflict. Find the give-and-take with students, compromise that elevates and encourages students in small ways and helps maintain a climate that is fun and friendly and earns student cooperation and even compliance in the moments when we most need it.

For me, this is the easiest part of teaching. I hope it is or becomes that for you, too.

Keeping Our Priorities Straight

I have seen teachers allow disruptive behavior to become personal. Sometimes, it is difficult not to. Those students are disrespecting not only our hard work and its mission but the educational needs of their peers. That is why we must *not* let it get personal.

Kids forget that the goal of our work is for their benefit. Their inner-conflicts and insecurities get played out as hostility aimed at us. They need to be reminded that we are there for them and their peers and that if we need to admonish them or sanction them in some way, it is not for our pride or ego—it is for the benefit of them and the other students. Never forget that, and never forget to remind students of that. Let the disruptors know that you will deal similarly with anyone who disrupts their learning. That your job is to protect them—from their counterproductive impulses and those of anyone else in the room.

That is really all most teenagers want from us—a commitment to act in their best interests. If we can convey those sentiments to them, we can not only help them past those impulses; we can also inspire peer pressure from other students to cooperate.

De-escalation

About a decade ago, I was invited onto a cable News show to talk about my experiences with classroom and school violence. The reporter or someone on his staff had read my book—or at least the part where I'd referred to being shot at and having confiscated weapons from students.

During the interview, taped remotely, I was asked about a series of video-taped classroom incidents that had gone viral in which teachers were being assaulted. The reporter seemed to be looking for my condemnation of this generation of urban public-school students, but I wasn't taking the bait. I attributed the problem to the lack of preparation and support for many teachers. I said that teachers who were willing and able to do the hard work of de-escalating student anger and frustration did not get assaulted, but that far too many teachers are overwhelmed and that the underfunding of schools is a big part of the problem. When the segment aired, none of that was included. Mostly they showed two other teachers from different cities who complained about student violence against them. They blamed negligent parents and rap music. One had already left the profession. The only part of my interview they showed was my response to questions about my experience being shot at and confiscating weapons.

The next day, another show on the same network invited me to do a phone interview. They promised it would be live, so I agreed, figuring they couldn't edit out any of what I said. They didn't—but while I spoke about how kids need adults who can help them calm down, adults they care about who are willing to help them in their worst moments, the show's producers were showing, on a loop, students of color attacking teachers.

The popular imagination seems to have been infected with the mythology of bad kids—out of control, incorrigible, feral monsters, a slightly softened rehash of the 1990s "super predator" fallacy.

The truth is that student conflict, verbal and physical, are almost entirely preventable if we can identify it in time and de-escalate. Seeing the antecedents of potential student conflict in its early stages is an acquired skill. Being able to hear the low rumble of student tension and intervening. Sometimes just having the students know that you know they are upset is enough to temper the fury and stop their thoughts from racing toward self-destruction. It helps immensely if we have established a rapport with students, though I have managed to calm and diffuse students I hardly knew. The greatest challenge in all of this is that no one ever trains us in how! I find this remarkable that, as a young teacher, this was something I had to figure out for myself.

We are also sometimes put in extremely stressful working conditions—big classes of challenged students in classrooms that are either too small with not enough seats or too hot or too cold and without adequate resources—especially when we are inexperienced. In such circumstances, it may not be easy for us to de-escalate our own stress, frustration, and anger, much less calm our students.

I wish this were not the case. It is shameful, and I can only say do the best you can, be patient with yourself, and take refuge in the fact that things do tend to get better for us as we become more effective, with experience, at de-escalation and everything else.

What I can also tell you, having survived long enough to become more effective, are some of the ways I have figured out, mostly on my own, to de-escalate student conflict and student meltdowns. I lead with empathy and compassion, sympathetic but also firm, letting kids know that their anger doesn't entitle them to hurt anyone.

Sometimes I use distraction. Get the students talking about their beef but try to steer them toward something else until they calm down. Other times I try humor. I even, sometimes, bore them into a stupor with a lesson in some related psychology or sociology or history. Mostly I just listen to them gripe and show patience and sympathy.

When students are upset at me, I let them complain. I don't mind being a receptacle for their anger—whether I was the cause of it or not. Either way, nothing to take personally. Just a way to support students who sometimes need to vent and may not have a lot of sympathetic ears available to them. They mostly appreciate the indulgence.

> In their worst moments, teenagers are lost children and what they often need more than anything is an adult to accept them for what they are in that moment and listen and also to expect more of them.

In their worst moments, teenagers are lost children and what they often need more than anything is an adult to accept them for what they are in that moment and listen and also to expect more of them.

No Front

Students also need, in their worst moments and pretty much all the time, to save face no matter what. They are enduring the most self-conscious time of their lives, and their social capital with peers is profoundly, desperately important. Every interaction we have with them is influenced by whether anyone can see or hear it.

For some kids, this condition manifests as abject shyness. Others crave attention and will try to humiliate someone, including us, if it might elevate their status. I have seen students cry and be vulnerable when they were alone with me and then, just hours or minutes later, ridicule me for the sake of peer approval or to conceal their own emotional vulnerability. It is a kind of twisted teenage expression of trust: they believe we understand them enough and care about them enough to let them get away with it in order to protect their image.

The students I teach call it "fronting" (or used to), showing up the teacher for the rep (another not-so-current expression). It is something many will do without compunction, especially if we are trying to correct their behavior, and for that reason, I have always tried to admonish students privately.

That means a whisper, a look, or else politely inviting them to step just outside or someplace where no one else will hear what I have to say and no one has to see them react. It means that if I want to talk to a student after class, I don't tell them that during class in front of their peers; I catch them on their way out and pull them aside. It means it's nobody else's business—and kids appreciate that.

Making that effort keeps them as allies, even those who seem to be determined to destroy us. If we maintain enough student allies, then peer pressure can work for us.

Dislocation Is the Very Last Resort

It is natural to want disruptive students removed from the classroom. If they appear not to be interested in learning, if they seem not to want to be there anyway, why should we and our other students be burdened? The answer is simple: because sending kids out of our room is an admission of our limitations and it is a rejection of kids who often are the ones who most need our support. I know school deans who, almost every day, entertain an office full of dislocated students. They are mostly boys—and in many schools they are disproportionately African American. Some spend more time with the dean than with any of their teachers.

Our goal, as teachers, should be to keep all our students with us and address disruptions ourselves. I say goal because things can get overwhelming, especially for new and struggling teachers, and no one ought to expect us to have the tools to deal with every student all the time. But I have seen struggling teachers get used to sending kids out and begin to rely on removal as their primary means of handling disruption. I have also heard administrators complain about such teachers and I have seen admins refuse to house those disruptors and instead send them back to the teacher who already showed they didn't want them around and didn't know how to help them. Unfair as it is, when we too readily send kids away, we begin a cycle of weakness and dependence that can escalate the problem.

What I say to those teachers is relax. Take the time to figure out how to deal with disruptors. Unfair as it may seem—that they can disrupt without punishment and that other students are losing precious learning time—if we are playing that long game of becoming effective teachers, our time is well-spent developing our skills at maintaining order, maintaining our composure, and resisting attempts to derail us. Meanwhile, even as we might believe we are losing instructional time, we are teaching our students, all of them, about patience, persistence, determination, humility, and the immense power of learning through trial and error.

There are, of course, times when you might have to send a student out—for safety or just everyone's peace of mind. Sometimes kids need separation from each other, at least temporarily, but when we do that we should always follow up with the kid and let them know we want to improve things. I have asked disruptive students for feedback about my teaching. To let them know they have as much right to judge me as I to judge them, and that I don't dislike or resent them. They are kids and should be allowed to mess up. I have even, at times, defended disruptive kids to their peers whose judgements are harsher than mine would ever be.

Indifference Ought Never Be an Option

It is understandable, during our most stressful and humiliating moments with students, to want to detach ourselves from them, but we must guard against indifference and never allow ourselves to express it.

Teenage Insecurities already have kids doubting our commitment and concern for them. Many of them, deep down, don't believe they deserve anything but our contempt—especially those who are causing us the most grief. They know they are a pain. Beneath their bravado and their own feigned indifference—that can produce such seeming hostility and cruelty toward others—is an exaggerated sense of self-perceived awfulness. I know this because of all the apologies I have received years later or even just days later. Students almost always remember their behavior as far worse than it seemed to me.

So I never even joke about indifference to them because I have learned that for some kids our concern feels like their only hope and the only reason why they should believe they are worth anything. I remind myself that my struggle, such as it is, is their lifeline. Some of our students have families that love and care about them, but others do not, and our indifference can be devastating.

In fact, the worse a student behaves, the more they probably need us to care. They may need us to express that concern by correcting their behavior and making them fully accountable for it, but always with some reminder that they are important to us. I have seen too many administrators kick a kid out of school (for fighting, extreme bullying, carrying a weapon, having drugs, whatever) with a cold shoulder and an attitude of—or even the actual words—"good riddance" and then gotten the news that kid had dropped out or been arrested, been killed in the street or died by suicide.

> In fact, the worse a student behaves, the more they probably need us to care.

You might have a student in your class who seems beyond any reasoning or hope. They might seem sociopathic. There do seem to be such people in the world and some of them must have once attended high school, but I have never taught anyone who seemed beyond hope, and I have taught students who were on probation for violent crimes, including at least one who was alleged to have committed a homicide. Read or watch a TED talk about Father Boyle's accounts of working with East L.A. gang members. Some of them were stone-cold killers—only it turned out they were just very traumatized kids.

Bad behavior is often a symptom of emotional pain, a cry for help. We must never under-estimate our impact on kids.

About Rules

Much of my education about being a teacher focused on establishing and enforcing class rules. Teachers are told to begin every school year by going over those rules, having students read them aloud and talking about them, and having students and their parents sign a contract agreeing to abide by them.

It seems a reasonable approach. Be clear about expectations, and then provide a policy of progressive consequences for those who violate them. It seems to work for some teachers. It seems especially useful for those who teach in a middle school, but I have known many high school teachers who also use that approach, and I know that a lot of administrators encourage it.

For me, though, it has always seemed counter-productive. For me, chasing after rule compliance seems to suggest to students that they are somehow under suspicion. Like being reminded in a store that there are cameras watching us and that shoplifters will be prosecuted, or as happens to many of my students when they go to the mall or the swap meet, being followed around by the clerk or the owner.

I remember on my first day as a teacher, how I'd composed a list of rules I was going to present to students but never handed it out or mentioned it. Somehow it just didn't feel right for me. Here, I was trying to establish some trust with these kids and then maybe build on that, and this list of rules and the contract that went with them seemed like a complete negation of trust. I ended up telling students there were only two rules:

- ♦ I respect them.
- ♦ In return, they respect me and each other.

Everything else would get worked out from that premise.

It hasn't been a seamless process, but that mutual respect has gone a very long way for me and the students I have had the honor of teaching.

21

We Are All Beginners

In a strange way, teaching has always, for me, been a lot like writing. Yes, writing is done largely in isolation, while teaching is intensely immersed in people and personality. But both endeavors are perpetually about discovery, especially self-discovery. They both require exhausting amounts of imagination. Perfection is elusive—if not impossible—for writers as well as teachers. Every time I embark on a newspaper column or a script or a book, much as I am informed by my experience as a writer, I am very much a beginner, trying to figure it all out. The same feels true about teaching.

When I was a student teacher, I was supervised by two "master teachers," a term I have come to believe is misleading. I owe a great debt to those two women, but it wasn't mastery they imparted to me; it was love and humility and a willingness to stay open-minded and figure things out. I have discovered for myself in the years since then that every class with its unique cohort of students presents new challenges. For that matter, every time I meet with a classroom of students, they have changed since the last time we met. So have I. With experience, the job of beginning anew gets easier and more manageable and less draining, but I do not believe there is anyone who can accurately be called a master teacher.

> With experience, the job of beginning anew gets easier and more manageable and less draining, but I do not believe there is anyone who can accurately be called a master teacher.

DOI: 10.4324/9781003538936-25

What we can hope for is to get comfortable with the awesome responsibility of teaching and develop the tools and temperament to respond to every teaching challenge, familiar or new.

The Lessons of Complacency

My first year as a full-time teacher, I carpooled with one of the veteran teachers at the school. She was very supportive and often helpful, but there was one thing she said to me several times that in retrospect seems misguided. She warned me about the hazard of becoming bored once I figured it all out.

I still appreciate that warning, though I have discovered that the needs, demands, and idiosyncrasies of students go a long way toward preventing boredom. I also try to keep refreshing what I teach and how I teach it to keep from getting stale. What I have never experienced is the part about figuring it all out.

There have been moments where I might have thought I had but they have been short-lived. I have learned the lessons of complacency and overconfidence. My students are very effective teachers in that regard, always finding new ways to humble me.

Reason to Be Humble and Proud

There is no end to what we can do for our students. Truly. There aren't enough hours in the day or days in the year to do all the preparation to elevate every second of every class into a customized, interactive, comfortable, and compelling experience for every student, and then provide all the feedback and attention and counseling they need. Maybe if we had five or ten students in a few classes a day but right now, as I write this, I have more than 200 students over seven classes and there is always more that I could do for them. Considering all that, it is an impossible job.

But I am committed to always seeking ways to do more for students without sacrificing my family life too much or burning myself out. In that regard, I am no different from the first-, second-, and third-year teachers I mentor. One thing I tell them all the time is that they are doing better, a lot better, than they think they are. The work of teachers does not all manifest in our students while they are in our classes. If we can make a career of teaching, though, we will get those letters and emails and visits attesting to the lasting impact we have made.

Part IV
All in for the Kids and Ourselves
Keeping the Fire without Being Consumed

22
Dispatching Demands and Weathering Fads

Nothing is more frustrating for a teacher than seeing all the time and energy and resources squandered on ridiculous requirements and misguided mandates that betray what are supposed to be the priorities of every school.

I have known teachers who left or almost left the profession because of this frustration. At the very least, all the petty nonsense is a potential distraction from the work of educating kids. To keep our outrage in check, we must develop a tolerance for stupidity while finding ways to dispatch all the useless demands.

Most of these outrages are not intentionally onerous. They are often the product of earnest attempts to improve things. The education system is quite good at transforming good intentions into burdensome absurdity. Our tormentors are only occasionally nefarious. Mostly, they just have a knack for taking some aspect of a good idea and ruining it—and vexing us in the process.

Assault by Lesson Plan

For most of us, a useful lesson plan is a rough outline, the structure and order of student learning activities with some notes, perhaps an approximate timeline of inputs and outcomes. This is entirely different from the formal lesson plans assigned in a teacher education class and which we are asked to produce for our administrators when they are going to officially observe and evaluate us.

Some administrators demand such formal lesson plans—and/or unit plans—on a regular basis. I have never met a teacher who finds this practice the least bit useful to effective teaching. Nor have I heard an administrator make a convincing argument for adding this burden to already overworked teachers. Their reasons for inflicting them on us vary. Among them are pressure from their supervisors, the need to justify themselves as instructional leaders, and the false belief that teachers are not self-motivated to do their best. There are teachers who need to be pushed, and formal lesson plan requirements may be a means to that end, and to avoid singling out specific teachers, many admins will punish the entire staff. It can seem sadistic to us or, at the very least, passive-aggressively vengeful. Admins were once teachers. They should know what they are putting us through.

I do not advise agonizing too much over the reason—or the requirement. I say get it over with as quickly and painlessly as possible and move on. Figure out a method, create your shortcuts.

If you are having a formal observation, make your rough lesson plan—the one you'll actually follow—and then spin it into your admin's template. Then hunker down and grind it out. If there is specific jargon they want, feed it to them. Use artificial intelligence software if you have to. Ditto for all the lesson plans you are required to submit to any admin. Be environmentally friendly to your soul—recycle and reuse these as much as necessary and as much as possible and change as little as you need to; keep it simple. As much as possible, save your time, mental energy, and creative talents for what will impact your students.

Does it make hypocrites out of us to use AI ourselves and then object to students exploiting these same kinds of shortcuts? Not at all. In both cases, we are working in the interest of student learning, keeping them honest so they really learn, protecting our time so we can devote it to what helps them.

I have known colleagues who respond to requests for formal lesson plans like a civil litigator burying an opponent in motions; these teachers submit massive and massively complex lesson plans—AI generated or copy-pasted from somewhere or other—and overwhelm their admins in words to ensure they will never read them and increase the probability that they will stop making such requests. I am not recommending that anyone do this, especially any teacher without seniority or job security; just something some teachers have used to reclaim time they can use for the benefit of students.

I have known teachers who turned in the same formal lesson plan every week for an entire school year and confirmed their admin wasn't reading any of them—and apparently neither was anyone else. Again, not a recommendation, just an observation. I have also known teachers who sincerely completed years of formal lesson plans and said they made useful discoveries about teaching. I have also known teachers unwilling to risk offending their admin with any shortcutting who sincerely completed weekly or even biweekly lesson plans and got faster and better at it and managed to survive the ordeal.

Board to Death

I began my teaching career, writing on a blackboard with white and sometimes yellow sticks of chalk that would roll off metal trays and shatter on the floor. I can still hear the clicks and shrieks of my letters and graphics, and smell that dust the eraser would waft into the rancid classroom air. Now, of course, we have whiteboards and erasable markers and a lot of us hardly use them anymore, favoring projectors and screens, smartboards and doc cams and other electronic media. Whatever we use, many of us will be required to post agendas with standards and other components of what is now, at least in some education circles, referred to as "whiteboard configurations."

It is not unreasonable to want students to know what they are going to have to do for the next 45 to 90 minutes of their lives and with some explanation why. There are teachers, particularly in middle school, who have students begin class by copying the agenda and standards as a grounding exercise, a transition from the between-classes-madness to learning mode. I have had a lot of conversations with students about their past teachers, the best and the worst, and no student has ever raved about copying an agenda or a standard. Nor have I seen many students get very excited or engaged upon seeing an agenda, not even when that agenda has the assurance that what they will be learning aligns with the Common Core.

There is nothing wrong with telegraphing the class, letting students know the plan, but also nothing wrong with surprising kids. As long as we know what we are doing and why, students will respond, and they will learn. The same is true about standards, Common Core or whatever comes next (something inevitably will). As long as we have a clear understanding of where our lesson fits in the continuum of our instructional plans, and we are coaxing students to think critically, challenging their assumptions, better understand what they read, better articulate their insights, and expand their knowledge of life and the universe, then our students will thrive. Meanwhile, maintaining teacher autonomy is far more meaningful—to our students and to us—than any fad whimsically mandated by people who spend little time working with kids.

> In fact, with the expertise of experience, we tend to need much less of an explicit plan and can be more responsive to the students in the room, collaborating with them to find the direction and pace of the class.

In fact, with the expertise of experience, we tend to need much less of an explicit plan and can be more responsive to the students in the room, collaborating with them to find the direction and pace of the class.

Thus, for many of us, these board configuration mandates are intrusive and oppressive. They can be a time-wasting drain on the creative energy of our classes. But they need not be. If we resist resisting. If we surrender to the inevitability and see it as an opportunity rather than a burden, we can create a board configuration that works for us and our students.

For me, it has become an interactive exchange with students on which I post ideas about what we might do, and they can respond with their input. I offer them a link to a shared document where they can offer more detailed ideas. Most students cannot be bothered, but they seem to appreciate the opportunity. I also post learning objectives and standards which students uniformly ignore, but which excite administrators and district officials when they enter the room—these board configurations, after all, are really more for them than anyone else. I also have my word of the day along with Oxford Dictionary words of the year from the past few years and some words that are good substitutes for students trying to cut down on their use of profanity and some humorous rules for writing. I also leave space for students to add, words, drawings, and cryptic pearls of their own wisdom—some of which are appropriate enough that I don't have to immediately erase them.

If it sounds like a lot of work, I should note that none of what I post is handwritten. I type these messages and print them on copy paper and use magnets to secure them to the board so that they cannot be erased and are easily replicable if necessary. I should also add that the "word of the day" is always the same. The word is *quotidian* (which, of course, means occurring every day). When students complain that I never change it, I tell them to look closely at the definition.

Most students pay little attention to my whiteboard configuration and, having devoted less than an hour to constructing it, neither do I.

PD and Meeting Survival

I used to think my close colleagues and I were the only teachers stricken with hours and hours (that felt like weeks and months) of mind-numbing and pointless professional development (PD) at the hands of our admins and whoever else they subjected us to. Now, thanks to social media, I know that we are not alone. Not even close. The PD teacher nightmare is, it seems, ubiquitous, and many teachers are speaking out about it, hilariously at times.

In my 34 years as a teacher, I have found a few PDs to be useful. I am grateful for them and sad that they are so rare.

I believe I can recall just about all of them. There was a mental health professional who spoke to our staff about children in crisis and best practices for helping them. Back in the 1990s and early 2000s, local law enforcement used to come in every year and tell us which nearby gangs were beefing and what colors and logos they were sporting and other updates for our safety and to help us keep our students safe and sane amid the mayhem. There have also been a few expert educators, former and still-working teachers, who delivered dynamic, insightful, innovative, and really useful presentations and interactive sessions that left a lasting impression.

Mostly, though, PD is a slog. It afflicts administrators who are mandated to provide their staff with thirty or forty or fifty hours a year of it, usually with limited financial resources, leaving them to improvise much of it. They end up just trying to fill time to meet the requirement. These admins would do well to let teachers figure out their own PD. Most teaching staff" are a wealth of knowledge, skill, and experience and everyone can learn from each other if given the chance, but I have never experienced that kind of trust and have never heard of it anywhere else.

Then there are the district PDs, most for compliance, rarely inspired, sometimes important, often superfluous.

Even PD for which our school and district pays outside vendors is mostly mediocre or miscalibrated to the audience. A few years ago, for example, one of the local universities was contracted to give us 20 hours of PD; we discovered early on that their expertise was K–5 and we knew far more than they did about teaching high school students.

There are quite a few ways to cope with bad PD. I do not recommend becoming outraged and launching an overt protest—and even getting confrontational with the presenters—something I have done more times than I should have. Trying to use the time to get work done is an obvious compromise, a covert protest and an expression of priorities. Marking papers, giving students written feedback, and discharging bureaucratic obligations are all good uses of time if you can manage to concentrate on it and not too seriously offend those admins.

Sometimes, after a long day in the classroom, it is hard to block out the soul-crushing nonsense and be productive. Sometimes the only defense against the insult is to privately mock the proceedings. I do not mean to suggest that teachers can be as mischievous as our most recalcitrant students, but learning is almost never a one-way street. I have seen teachers passing notes. I have been privy to PD group chats. I think the most innovative response might be playing PD bingo by making bingo cards, randomly filing each box with brief descriptions of likely occurrences—use of a buzz word or phrase, the sleepy teacher falling asleep, the complainer complaining, the likes-to-hear-themselves-talk teacher asking a dumb question, and so on. Just make sure no one hollers "BINGO" if they win.

Speaking of dumb questions—and questions in general—someone has to lean on anyone who asks a question during the last 15 minutes of a PD, especially when it looks like it might end a little early.

I have done that leaning on and I have rebelled in pretty much every way against bad PD, but my strongest advice to any new teacher is actually to approach PD always with a positive attitude. I try to see it all as an opportunity for something meaningful. I have actually managed, at times, to hijack a PD into a discussion of something useful and even urgent. I do not believe that the people who generate PD wish to aggravate us or waste our time, and so I believe I am helping them by derailing the aggravating waste of time into something productive. I try to inspire others to do the same.

I could write an entire section about staff meetings, but I have found the lines quite blurry between PD and meetings. I am told that some admins disdain the regular meetings and try to always communicate almost everything via email, but I think most of us are not that lucky. Again, I advise a positive attitude of hope toward productivity, but don't be afraid to being up what really matters, whether it is on the agenda or not—as long as you don't extend the meeting. Mocking the proceedings can earn our administrator's contempt; advocating for what ought to matter in the school will more likely gain their respect, whether they like it or not.

Other Time Wastes and Aggravations

Having to cover classes can be monumentally annoying, especially when the assignment is last minute and not for additional pay. If your classroom is available during your prep period, bring the class you are covering back to your room so you don't have to get acclimated to someone else's space and to remind students that you are a teacher at the school and might, at some point, be theirs.

I try to always have some generic lesson plan and handouts ready in case there are no plans or instructions left for the class. Kids will often claim they have nothing from the class to work on. Sometimes that is true, but start to hand out your assignment and they may suddenly remember an assignment not yet completed. As with everything else, always approach it with a positive outlook. Covering a class can be an opportunity to get to know our students better and a chance to try new instructional approaches. You never know when something great will happen.

I try to have the same optimism with other annoyances. Like a twice-a-week advisory period, created for the convenience of admins and counselors in case they want to hold an assembly or make a presentation to students. Most days it is an unstructured half hour of trying to make students listen to PA announcements, then create some meaningful activity that is usually interrupted by roving announcements or kids being summoned to the attendance office. Still, I am always looking for ways to make something meaningful happen, even if it is just teaching them how to play backgammon or chess or holding a Scrabble tournament.

Returning to campus toward the end of the pandemic, we were told to spend this advisory period on "social emotional learning." Addressing student social and emotional needs is vital and something that should be a part of everything we do. Telling us to shoehorn it into a specific time period was misguided and potentially self-defeating—and even possibly cringy. Still, a positive attitude and a little creativity helped some of us kind of make it work.

A little positivity can even save us the cringe-fest jargon and their buzz words that infect our schools and school systems, the linguistic catastrophe that is education speak. If you can embrace the jargon, good for you. If, like me, you find it nauseating, the good news is that our students are most immune to it, and they are who matter and who we spend the vast majority of our time with. The rest can become the white noise we get used to.

Finally, I must tell you to beware of burdens disguised as honors and opportunities. Like the coordinatorship that offers a token amount of extra pay in exchange for endless extra hours and compliance pain. If you have administrative ambitions, such agony might be worth it; otherwise, consider very carefully. Even a chance to spend part of a grant can turn into a nightmare. I watched a drama teacher and a music teacher become suffocated in bureaucratic folly trying to get equipment and materials to enrich their classes. They never actually got any of what they wanted or needed. The disorganization of the district staff overseeing the grant and the obscure and seemingly arbitrary grant guidelines pushed both teachers over the edge. The music teacher ended up on a four-month stress leave; for the drama teacher, the ordeal was a contributing factor in an early retirement.

Whatever does manage to get your ire, try to remember that most educators, at their core, mean well and really do want the best for kids. The unrealized potential of our schools can be enraging, or it can inspire us to try and push things, at least slightly, in the right direction. Doing that can keep us focused on what matters, and maybe we help a few others achieve the same focus and objective. It can also help us to always stay empathetic with our students who suffer the greater brunt of all the inefficiencies, corruptions, and absurdities.

23
Try to Be an Ally with Admins

One might imagine, based on the previous chapter and other things I have written, that I am uniformly contemptuous of administrators.

Far from it.

I have worked with many smart, committed, courteous, and supportive principals and assistant principals. That is why I tend to be impatient with those admins who prove peevish, petty, and pusillanimous. Even then, acrimony accomplishes nothing, and I have seen the harm caused when teachers and admins are at odds. It disquiets kids, who always manage to sense such antipathies, and it can be a huge distraction for teachers. It undermines our common purpose and breaks down communication, rendering the school less efficient and effective.

Needless to say, admins should lead the way toward maintaining harmony. Teachers have every right to protect ourselves professionally and advocate for students. But when admins fall short of their leadership responsibilities, as pathetic and unfair as that is, we are, in the long run, better off if we can carry the burden and make the effort to minimize conflict for the sake of the kids we teach.

Empathy Serves Us

We do not owe administrators our empathy—and it might seem bizarre to suggest we develop any, especially if those admins seem mostly aloof to our struggles. Actually, the reasons for doing it are self-serving.

As with any boss, our understanding of their job and its challenges can help us get the most out of them, advocating for students with them and protecting ourselves from their abuses of power. At the very least, our understanding of them can assist us in managing expectations.

Administrators have an often thankless job. They are under pressure from above—the assistant principals (or vice principals as they are sometimes called) must answer to the principal, who in turn answers to everyone above them in the district hierarchy. Administrators are supposed to be instructional leaders, but much of their time gets consumed with operational concerns, financial crunches, custodial crises, safety snafus, parental pressures, and on and on. Admins are regular receptacles of complaints from students, teachers, parents, the people who live adjacent to the campus, coaches, rival coaches and parents, law enforcement, etc. Their interactions with students are often unpleasant and involve misconduct.

Being an administrator sometimes requires upsetting people. They have to settle disputes and often must do so in ways that piss everyone off. They have to deliver bad news to parents about their children. This task does not suit everyone's temperament, so it can be a job filled with dread. Many admins work in a constant state of anxiety, trying to manage one crisis after another, hoping they aren't about to get a call from an angry superior.

I do not have an abundance of sympathy for them, nor do I believe any of us owe them more than what constitutes basic human decency. Our jobs can be at least as stressful, sometimes because of them. Administrators chose to leave the classroom for the desk and the walkie-talkie, the ring of keys, and, in most cases, the larger salary. If they tire of all that, they can always return to teaching.

Still, understanding their challenges can help us measure our expectations against what we can realistically expect from them. It can also be essential to compelling them to act in our interests and those of our students. One of the first lessons of the

AP Language class I teach is how much any argument relies on identifying the audience and then framing the line of reasoning in terms of what matters to them.

When we need something from our admin, we are far more likely to get it if we can find a way to align it to a need or concern of theirs—raising test scores, increasing graduation rates and college matriculation, reducing student suspensions and other disciplinary actions, getting parents off their backs, etc.

> Supporting the administrative agenda, as long as we can do it without interfering with student learning and well-being (theirs and ours), is always worth the effort.

Supporting the administrative agenda, as long as we can do it without interfering with student learning and well-being (theirs and ours), is always worth the effort. It can also constitute a down payment on whatever we might at some point need from an administrator.

We are all supposed to share the priority objective of student success. Politics, ambition, and fatigue may obscure the goal, but we all know the purpose of the school and why we are there being paid a salary. Teachers and admins may measure student success differently—we tend to see the challenges and progress up close in human terms, and most districts make sure that admins are drunk on data—but it is often not so difficult for us to find common ground in our generally common interest.

Trust with Caution

Administrators operate in a political sphere where fear and loathing and paranoia can corrupt even the most earnest educator. The adversarial nature of districts and teacher unions can corrode interactions between administrators and us, and many admins are conditioned to distrust and distance themselves from teachers. They sometimes view us as one of many school resources and set about getting the most out of us. That may sound consistent with a teacher's goal of effective instruction, but that is not always the case.

Still, the most effective administrators are the ones with an open mind and a healthy respect for the work we do with students, and a desire to help us do it better. If we offer them a positive belief in their intentions, they might ultimately reciprocate. Smart leaders understand the value of our trust and want to nurture it.

Expressing our trust means telling admins what we think and feel about our work, their work, and the culture and direction of our school. It means honoring our word and believing in theirs. It means being unafraid to respectfully and constructively criticize their leadership. It means discussing our instructional work candidly and honestly and being open to feedback from them.

It has to be a two-way street, and there is only so far we can reasonably extend ourselves if an administrator cannot offer mutual respect or trust. But if we are stricken with an adversarial administrator, at least we will know that we offered something that would have elevated our school's culture and the well-being of our students.

In more than 30 years, I have rarely found myself in that circumstance. When I find myself at odds with admins, it is most often the result of their fears and pressures and their inability or unwillingness to transcend them. In those cases, there is always the possibility of compromise. Trust can enable that compromise. That is why it is worth the time and effort to build that trust.

Meet on Common Ground

Experience has taught me that administrators and teachers really can be partners with a shared vision.

Ideally, it is the admin whose leadership finds that common ground. Realistically, it may be up to us to show that leadership and, in so doing, help an administrator become a better leader. I actually have had the privilege of being part of an admin's growth, a teacher mentoring an AP, ironic as that may sound. But why not? If we want effective, fair, and insightful admins, they really need

> If we want effective, fair, and insightful admins, they really need to learn from us.

to learn from us. Learning always goes in both directions; those experiences have made me a better teacher.

Our common objective should never be difficult to remember. If we show administrators that we are fully committed to kids—that we aren't driven by ego or vanity, and that we are reasonable toward students and have no interest in being gatekeepers of their success—we are more than likely to earn their respect and trust and might even inspire a deeper commitment on their part.

Be Reasonably Helpful

Our common objective should compel admins to support us—and it ought to make us want to support them.

They need our input, whether or not they seek it or appreciate it, and giving it can be advantageous to us. Offering it to them is an affirmation of our value beyond our classroom.

To be clear, I do not believe in offering admins my time without compensation, but in a crisis moment, I will do what I can for students, their parents, and any other stakeholders. When there are important decisions to make, I will offer my insight and expertise.

Some years ago, ethnic tension at our school manifested in several ugly incidents. It was a crisis for everyone who cared about students and cared about the culture of our school. I had seen similar conflicts at our school in previous years and had some insight into what it would take to restore harmony and move toward a deeper understanding between students. I also had the trust of some of the students at the forefront of the hostilities and could mediate, without judgment or the threat of punishment, and convince those students to make the effort to work things out. It was a teachable moment. It was a moment when I had administrators' backs. I was also able to pass on some complaints to those admins who had the opportunity to rethink how they were treating various students and let them know just how closely kids scrutinized every interaction with them and how sensitive they were to slights and favoritism.

On another occasion, I was attending what was supposed to be a student's final IEP meeting before graduation. This young man was graduating near the top of his class and had been accepted to a fairly competitive university despite his autism. The admins and psychologists seemed to assume this meeting would be little more than a formality and a celebration and were almost immediately blindsided when, through an interpreter, the young man's mother began listing complaints, claiming her son had been short-changed and threatening legal action. No one seemed to know how to respond to her other than to dispute her claims and get her even more riled up. I thought I understood what was going on, having watched my own parents struggle over my developmentally disabled brother. I texted the AP and counselor, who were sitting right across from me, and explained that the young man's mother was probably having apprehensions that her son was about to end the only positive school experience he'd ever had (he'd been bullied and isolated prior to our school). Unrealistic as it might have been, this woman wanted her son's positive experience to continue. She wanted the district-provided support to keep going. I told the AP to start helping her figure out how to get support for him in college and maybe, in the meantime, offer a few more sessions with the psychologist and other specialists. The AP read the text and turned the meeting around and averted a confrontation that could have ended up in the district's legal department.

Not all admins are open to our advice. Sometimes, the administrative ego tells them that no teacher could have much of value to tell them. Other admins just want to keep their distance for the sake of the hierarchy and some admins are wary of being in any way indebted to a teacher.

The smart and secure ones have no such reservations, and I have even, at times, found myself being confided in by admins about professional and personal struggles. Those of us who are listeners—who can offer a non-judgmental ear—can transcend some of the hierarchical absurdities of school leadership structures. Like Nick in *The Great Gatsby*, I am wary of such "intimacies" from school administrators and certainly don't go looking for anyone to confide in me, but I also remain open and willing to listen.

A collegial relationship can make our job infinitely more pleasant and our school a more collegial place.

Treat Them as an Equal

Some among the administrative ranks tend to place teachers as inferiors based on job status, pay, and political power—and most districts probably support this hierarchy. Teachers, on the other hand, have reason to see things the opposite way. We have a greater impact on the people who matter most in the school; the work we do is the very purpose of the school.

Students benefit when we and the admins recognize our common objective, share a deep concern for our students, and see each other as equal partners in the mission of the school.

Mutual respect and an insistence on our equality is a powerful way of affirming our vital role, reminding admins of our value and importance and that their most important role is to support our work. It is worth repeating continually and emphasizing to them for their sake and for the sake of students who need to be reminded, sometimes every day, that their learning and academic success are our priority and ought to be theirs. Whether or not the institution truly reflects that. Getting students to believe in their importance can be the most powerful way to push back against institutional alienation and to help admins realize their potential and integrity as authentic and honest educational leaders.

Whatever Happens Keep It Positive

Even administrators who unambiguously favor their ambitions over what is best for kids can be coaxed into at least pretending to care and acting in good faith for the sake of their professional reputations if we vigorously and relentlessly—and politely—push the real priorities.

Every educator knows we are supposed to put the needs of students first. That isn't always easy—especially when student needs are in conflict with each other and when time and other resources are limited—but whenever we are making decisions of any kind, someone should always be asking how it will benefit students and if our admins aren't asking it, we do well to give them the benefit of the doubt and politely remind them of that governing principle as if they know and believe it.

Just as we can help students out of a conflict, if we offer them a path to peace and calm on which they can save face, we can persuade or at least influence admins in the right direction if we are patient, persistent, and positive.

Such generosity on our part ought not to require us to leave ourselves vulnerable to exploitation or deceit. I am not a fool—at least, I try to remember not to be. We should always protect ourselves and our students from the potential abuses of a disingenuous administrator.

I have often discovered, though, that self-protection can be compatible with respect, collegiality, and positivity. Even the most political and transactional administrator can be rendered more useful to teachers and students with a modest degree of trust and a willingness to agree upon shared goals.

24

Try Being a Partner with Parents

For many struggling teachers, there are at least a few students who present formidable challenges. Restless, Reluctant to participate in class, sometimes disrespectful or outright defiant, these kids can make us miserable, especially when we lack the skill or confidence to contain their behaviors and help them rise above their angst, anxiety, and agitation. We end up saying their names over and over in class and often repeating the names to our spouses, partners, and families.

In our most beleaguered moments, it is easy to start building a case against the parents of these kids.

> *What kind of parenting malpractice has produced such incorrigible children?*
> *If the parents did a better job, we could more reasonably do our jobs.*

An understandable sentiment but not very productive—and not always entirely accurate.

To be sure, there is a lot of less-than-exemplary parenting. I know—I've helped raise three children and I was far from perfect at it. Among the many other indignities of parenting, my own kids always seemed to mimic my worst flaws without hinting at having been influenced by any of my strengths. For what it's worth, they have all flipped that around in adulthood—which is no great revelation; we already know teenagers are not typically the best version of themselves.

Children are not always a reflection of their parents, especially during adolescence. There are good parents whose kids behave badly as teenagers. Sometimes, we can attribute at least some of that behavior to circumstance—trauma and loss—but sometimes, it is simply the enormous stresses of those years.

There are also parents limited by their own circumstances—poverty, distressed marriages, illness, as well as the demands of other children and other relatives suffering mental illness, other illnesses, substance abuse, and so on. Some of our students don't have stable parents or any parents. There are, of course, parents about whom we, as mandated child abuse reporters, must alert the authorities. For those kids we may be the only chance for positive adult relationships.

Whatever the circumstances, there isn't much constructive value in trying to assign blame for a student's shortcomings. What does benefit us, our students, and their families, when possible, is effective communication, empathy, positivity, and respect for parents or whoever else is trying to raise the children we are trying to teach.

Communication Is Key

Open communication with parents can be a powerful way to learn more about our students, to reassure parents of our commitment to their children, and to hold kids accountable. It is also, if you have anything close to the 200 or more students I usually have in my classes, a massive undertaking, one about which we've got to be reasonable with ourselves and insist on realistic expectations from administrators and parents. If I attempted to call every parent of every student at the beginning of the term, and each call averaged five minutes—and calls to parents can sometimes take much longer—it would amount to nearly 17 hours!

What I am willing to do is respond within twenty-four hours to parent emails, phone messages, or requests for a conference. I also provide my mobile phone number to parents who contact me or who attend back-to-school or parent/teacher conference evenings. Not everyone is comfortable giving out their number to parents—and that is a personal choice—but the gesture goes a long way toward building trust and mutual respect, and in all the years I've been teaching, no parent has ever done anything to make me regret it.

There are reasonable ways to reach out to all the parents of students in our classes. Mass Emails or other electronic messages can be useful for conveying information. Classroom newsletters are a way to let parents know what is going on in class and feature student work and accomplishments. I have used this tool at various times and have found that praising students in a public document is a powerful motivator. While less time-consuming than trying to call every parent, communicating via class newsletter is still a burden, especially to those of us with five or six or seven classes of more than 30 students each, and unless someone is paying us extra for that time, no admin or anyone else ought to expect us to do it.

It is ideal for us to establish trust and rapport with parents before problems arise with their child. The infuriating reality, though, is that schools don't give us the time to accomplish this. Instead, we almost always make our first contact with parents when their child is struggling or when we are struggling with their child. Such calls can be unpleasant for us and the parent, but they don't have to be.

Empathy Can Be Our Most Effective Tool

Being a parent has never been easy, and anyone who is one probably remembers when their kids were in high school. Parenting is an immensely challenging role, often thankless, especially during the first decades of the journey. Thankless and spiked with other people's judgments. Parents get critiqued by their own parents and other family and by friends, those with and without kids, by strangers in public places, bosses and co-workers, and, of course, by the children they are parenting.

Parenting can be profoundly meaningful and hopefully joyful, but it is also exhausting, time-consuming, sometimes tedious, vexing, financially destabilizing, and potentially heartbreaking, and a lot of us worry that we are doing a lousy job at it.

For some parents, the adolescence of their children is shocking, terrifying, and emotionally devastating. It can almost feel as if your sullen—or at least distant—teenager has kidnapped and murdered that bright and open child they used to be.

Of course, what we are witnessing is the pain of growing up—shared intimately by parents (and shared to some degree by teachers). Not just the physical pain of stretching bones and skin and tearing muscle fibers to rebuild them stronger but the breaking down of thinking structures to rebuild the mind for survival as an adult.

The worst of it can happen beyond the control of parents who suffer the brunt of the adolescent angst. They don't need judgment or contempt from teachers. They can use a little compassion and some encouragement. The best way to do that is to see some good in their child and show that we really care about them. I have had parents cry and plead with me to help their kid. Mostly parents are silently hoping.

Keeping It Positive

> If we see ourselves as partners with our students in their learning and growth and, by extension, partners with their parents who more than share that goal, we can approach parents in a positive way.

If we see ourselves as partners with our students in their learning and growth and, by extension, partners with their parents who more than share that goal, we can approach parents in a positive way. Most of them want to know how their child is doing in school. What no parent wants to hear—and what most fear coming from a teacher or admin—is that their child is somehow, whether we use the word or not, "bad."

Teachers who call to complain about a student will sometimes reach a parent who is able to influence that student, but that teacher should know that there is also a chance that parent's influence is limited. We shouldn't be surprised if parents shut down on us or get defensive. We also shouldn't be too hopeful that this time they will get results.

An alternative is to always lead with something positive about the student, something we like about them, something that indicates potential to be successful. It shouldn't be difficult for us; seeing the good in our students, even at their worst, is an essential skill for teachers.

Approaching parent communication with a positive stance changes the dynamic of the interaction. It opens parents to listening and wanting to help, especially if they perceive us as wanting to help them and their child. Show patience. I have found it extremely productive to reassure parents about their kids, that I believe in time they will improve, even when those kids are making my job harder every day. When parents feel overwhelmed by our concerns and complaints, they can end up alienating their child, and we, as instigators of that pressure, can alienate them, too.

I have never asked a parent to correct a student's behavior. To me, that feels insulting—it implies that they endorse the behavior or that they don't care. There may be some—a few—parents who don't care, but if that is the case, they are unlikely to accommodate us anyway.

I have tried, instead, to let parents know that we are in this together, that I share their disappointment and promise to do what I can to help. I share some of my own parenting struggles and how my own children overcame some of their challenges. I talk about former students who turned themselves around.

I find this approach gets far more action from parents and accomplishes something even more vital. When parents and teachers are truly partners—when a student hears positive words from parents about a teacher and from a teacher about their parents—they tend to feel more secure about themselves and their lives. This is always true when students are the children of former students. They already know we are partners and have a high regard for each other. Those students almost always do well in class.

I have encountered parents who anticipate the negative. They will ask me if their child is misbehaving or being disrespectful.

These are opportunities to talk about a student's academic strengths and weaknesses and gain insights that can inform my teaching. At a parent/teacher conference some years ago, a mother told me, "If Stanley gives you any problems, let me know and I will hurt him." Her pledge concerned me, but Stanley was so much bigger than his mom that I didn't think there was much potential for child abuse. Stanley could be a challenge in class at times, but I am not inclined to complain to parents. Instead, I told her everything I liked about Stanley, who was right there to hear it. From then on, whenever Stanley gave me a problem, I would say to him, "What would your mom say to you right now?" Usually, that was enough. If not then, I would make a big fuss about him, channeling some of that maternal guilt on behalf of his mom. It often worked with Stanley and speaking on behalf of a parent has worked well with others since then, and it is another good reason to get to know parents well enough to speak for them.

At another conference a few years later, I met with a man who didn't believe that I had nothing negative to say about his son. It was kind of sad. Raul wasn't perfect, but he was smart, hard-working, and mostly cooperative. The father kept pressing me for something bad about his son. I found it hard not to have contempt for this man and his stern parenting, but for all I knew, he was looking for an excuse not to buy Raul something promised that he couldn't really afford. More likely the man was just afraid if he wasn't tough enough on his son, he would somehow weaken the young man and set him up for failure. I promised Raul's father that I would be demanding of his son and that I would report to him any flaws in his performance. I did not think there would be a reason to, and there never was.

Parents Are Parents

I have spent the entirety of my teaching career in inner-city Los Angeles and have never taught children from privileged backgrounds. I have heard some private school colleagues complain about what they describe as overly entitled parents, arrogant and demanding. I have known some of those people in my personal life.

I do not envy teachers who must contend with the most aggressively entitled and demanding parents, but I have cautioned private school teachers who have confessed to me a bitterness and contempt that sometimes impacts their interactions with students. It may be understandable under the circumstances but there is never any excuse for abandoning our commitment to kids, however privileged or arrogant they and their parents are. We ought not underestimate our potential influence on our students and, through them, on a lot of others who are not so privileged or entitled.

Kids do not choose their parents and can do little to control them. Challenging parents are often a much greater burden to their children than to us, and if we approach any parent in a positive manner, we are more likely to forge a partnership and an understanding. If we reserve judgment and avoid blaming parents for their children's misdeeds, we actually leave the parents' room to realize just how appalling their kid's conduct is. They may still choose to justify it, but we don't have to waste time on intractable parents. Whether or not any parent is willing or able to assist us in that way, never give up trying to work with their child. We cannot always rely on the partnership of parents. All teachers do well to be prepared for that. It may seem absurdly unfair that we have to teach any teenagers basic decency and mentor and parent them along with providing a challenging and compelling curriculum. But this is what we've signed up for, and our unreserved commitment to kids elevates them and us.

For me, the most challenging parents are those whose religious or ideological beliefs put their kids at odds with them. Our job is to serve students and, by extension, their parents, but those dual objectives are not always compatible. In the most egregious instances, in which there is suspected child abuse, our obligation is a legal one to protect students. But when a student has an opportunity for an out-of-state college scholarship, and their parents give a hard "No," or when an LGBTQ+ student is afraid to come out to parents who are continually condemning the very identity the child is realizing about themselves, any support we offer that child may well be an affront to those parents.

I should say that, mostly, when students complain to me about their parents, I express respect for all parents and remind them how difficult parenting is. I sometimes offer them a parental point of view and always try to encourage empathy and understanding. But I have also opposed parents about interracial friendships and relationships, gender double standards, and, back in 2021, whether it was safe and sensible to receive the Covid-19 vaccine.

Such advocacy is, of course, beyond the job description. It can be risky though it can also help build trust and credibility with students. So, by the way, can standing up for parents, when appropriate, to students and administrators. I would never expect a colleague to do any of this. Such risks are a personal choice and sometimes a very difficult choice among the many difficult choices teachers have to make.

A veteran colleague from my early years used to muse ironically, "That's why they pay us the big bucks."

25

Protecting Kids from Travesty of Test Mania

Measuring student learning is essential, and effective teachers do it every day, but school districts and departments of education, on behalf of the taxpayers who fund the whole endeavor, need objective ways to arbitrate our success, so it seems there must be standardized tests. We can debate the efficacy of different types of these instruments. We can complain (and I often do) about multiple-choice tests that purport to measure a student's "writing" ability or writing tests scored by soulless machines or the general quality of some tests, badly worded and outright ambiguous test questions and downright erroneous answers. But standardized testing will probably always be a part of our lives as teachers. Hopefully, the companies that make them will continue to improve on their effectiveness.

My biggest doubt about this billion-dollar enterprise is that as students get older, the tests seem more a measure of their willingness to submit to standardized evaluations than their ability to perform on them. The smarter the student, I have observed, the more likely they are to figure out that the tests matter to everyone except them. There are exceptions, such as the New York State Regents tests, but mostly the perceived success of teachers and schools and districts is placed at the mercy of student mood and temperament.

Motivate Effort

This one is never easy. I am even, at times, ambivalent, especially when kids are being over-tested and I can see and hear and feel their fatigue. But I know that no one in positions of power cares much about any of that, and I want student scores to reflect their abilities.

Admins at the school where I teach have periodically required students with low test scores to attend after-school tutoring and Saturday school as an incentive to give maximum effort to those high-stakes tests. They seemed to have some success with those threats, but the most egregious test-resistors turn out to be the ones least likely to show up after school or on Saturdays—and least afraid of whatever threats are tied to that.

Now that most standardized tests are digital and results can sometimes be instantaneous, we can incentivize effort by factoring a student's test score into their class grade. Whenever using this, I have had to use a modified grading scale so as not to punish students who have learning challenges or just aren't good at taking tests. Of course, not all students care about their grades. Those ultra-apathetic students have always occupied a special place in my heart—probably because, in my early years as a struggling teacher, they were the kids who taught me the most about how to be an effective teacher. In fact, much as they may sometimes annoy me, they continue to be my most meaningful inspiration.

It may be that inspiration that has helped me realize there are valuable lessons for students in overcoming their inclination for silent, passive protest motivated by testing fatigue.

Evidence of that fatigue is easy to find—students rushing through these tests and scoring three or five or more grades below their actual abilities (a few years ago, a really bright tenth grader scored at kindergarten level). I am not unsympathetic to their frustration or the temptation to make a mockery of these tests. What I tell them is this:

> *Pick your battles. You may have some degree of justification for mocking the test, but there are so many serious injustices in the world, in your community, and even, perhaps, in your school.*

This is not the one to protest. The protest itself is self-defeating since sabotaging our school's results undermines your credibility with those in charge. On the other hand, do your best on this annoying test, score as high as you can, and then make demands.

I have also told students the ways in which these tests do matter—with, perhaps, some slight exaggeration: *Schools are ranked based on data that includes your test scores. Colleges pay attention to these rankings. Our school gets a high percentage of students into UCLA and other competitive universities. What do you think would happen if our school's scores took a nosedive?*

The answer is: I don't know if UCLA or any other college really cares about our standardized test scores, but I think it seems a reasonable argument to say that our school's academic reputation matters.

These are messages I have had to deliver over and over, and still, I find myself mostly at the mercy of each student's willingness to care. In that sense, performance on these tests is, as much as anything, a measure of how willing students are to go out of their way for their teachers. The best way to persuade students is to show a willingness to go out of our way for them. It begins the first day of school with how we welcome them to our class and with the hard work we do to make the class interesting, engaging, and fun, and make every student feel seen and appreciated, understood, and most of all, give every student a path to success.

There is no special trick to this. It's just good teaching—working hard and being fully committed to our students.

Support the Effort to Improve Test Scores

However successful we are at incentivizing students to give us reliable test data, and however much we are annoyed by the whole testing circus—the administrative hysteria, the shameful disruption of it all—we are wise to always support the effort, if not in our hearts then at least with our words and actions.

Pushing back against the tests themselves is even less useful for us than for our students. We should never allow ourselves to become the enemy of what matters to our admins or the district for which we work. If you act even slightly cynical about the testing enterprise, if you complain about how lame the tests are, you risk alienating those in charge, who may assume you are hostile to the test because you fear you have not adequately taught your students.

If we show support for the effort, we will exude confidence as teachers. We will also have the credibility to criticize the way the tests are administered—how many hours each day, where and by whom. I have, at times, gone so far as to suggest to admins that students would be more motivated on the tests if admins and other staff were more respectful and polite toward those students and less suspicious of them. Perhaps most important for us, our support of the testing effort and our commitment to maximizing student performance can enable us to be taken seriously when we refuse to willingly replace real teaching with test prep.

Test Prep Is Not Real Teaching

The summer that I worked at a New York City charter school, I discovered that all of my colleagues were also from somewhere else. I assumed everyone at this school just wanted the summer off, but found out, several weeks in, that just a few weeks prior the entire staff had been terminated.

Had there been an embezzlement scandal?
Or grades fixed for a rogue basketball coach?
Children exploited or mistreated?

No, no, and no; the board of that school had fired everyone because test score goals had not been met.

I do not know how low those test scores were or whether, for any reason, those teachers deserved to be terminated, but I have heard similar stories around the country, and I suspect that these drastic measures were misguided and misanthropic.

Indeed, top-down test anxiety is real, and it can be destructive.

Not just because it can create job instability for teachers—mostly those without strong unions. When those in power in schools get drunk on test data, they can end up, in the name of numerical improvement, sabotaging our classes by pushing to convert compelling curriculum, passionately produced, into lifeless test prep.

Testing is not teaching/Testing is not learning. Teaching to a test is not education. It is also not ethical. It is manipulation. It is the abandoning of what ought to be the mission of every school. At best, it is a capitulation to the craven impulses of the cynical and the political; at worst, it is the exploitation of our students for the sake of professional ambition and vanity.

> Testing is not teaching/Testing is not learning.

I decided long ago that I was going to teach students what I knew was important—prepare them for success—and have confidence that dedicated, passionate, and smart teaching would be reflected in student performance on whatever test was put in front of them. The challenge in that has been periodically convincing administrators to believe in me and our students.

I have been lucky. I began teaching long before the nadir or test mania and I taught for years at a school for at-risk students that flew largely under the district radar—before digital education management made that impossible. So that by the time I was pushing back against efforts to impose the tyranny of the test on everything we do in the classroom, I had the credibility, and the seniority to go along with membership in a strong union.

When administrators handed me photocopies of the previous year's test questions, I could hand them right back. When an admin told my colleagues and me to "backwards plan"—to align every lesson and assignment to some aspect of the test—I could ignore them and eventually tell them it wasn't necessary, and if they wished to reassure themselves, they could visit my classroom and see that I was providing a fun, meaningful, and comprehensive college-prep curriculum.

And if an administrator ever forced the issue, I was free to politely and respectfully tell them how ethically abhorrent it would be to stop teaching kids to enjoy and appreciate reading and develop a literary and rhetorical voice, to cease nurturing curiosity, skepticism, and originality, and the love of learning in favor of wrote drilling of multiple choice test taking in an effort to reduce adult anxieties about student test scores meeting the target goals that seemed to have replaced any passion they might have ever had about educating kids.

But, again, I am in a position to stand up to the affront. If I were a new teacher today, I would probably tread lightly, at least for a few years. I might express sadness, rather than disgust, at the cost to students of those cynical calculations. I might even suggest that the test prep will fail anyway since it alienates students and makes them tired of the tests before they are even supposed to take them.

Mostly, I would find a way, subversively, to provide students with as much authentic, fun, and interesting teaching as possible, and hope it inspires kids to try harder on those damn tests.

Some administrators themselves are skeptical of the test-score hysteria or at least not so afflicted as to afflict teachers. I hope you have the good fortune to work for some of them. I am also hopeful that this suffocating emphasis on standardized testing may be waning. Most colleges and universities are test-optional for the SAT and ACT, and some schools and districts are reconsidering how much testing kids should be subjected to.

Something all of us can do is be sure we are adequately and accurately measuring the progress of our students as part of our teaching and that our assessments of them are influencing what we teach and how we teach it. If we are ever going to convince administrators and school districts and politicians to stop funding the testing industrial complex, it will be, at least in part, because we demonstrated that we are successfully tracking student progress ourselves.

26

Don't EVER Lose Your Sense of Humor

My first days as a full-time teacher were terrifying, confounding, and exhausting. I felt completely at the mercy of students. Most were nice when I talked to them outside of class, one-on-one, but as a group, most were unmanageable. They would hurl themselves into the classroom and then swirl around in a chaotic storm. It seemed to take every ounce of strength to get their attention, and then sometimes, right at that moment, two kids would start yelling at each other about something or rise up to fight. At times, I felt hopeless.

When I handed out my expectations and goals for the class, I spoke passionately about my love of books and how they possessed the secrets of the universe, the keys to understanding each other and ourselves, and how self-expression through writing was the ultimate act of liberation. A hand went up in the back of the room. A young man in a blindingly white T-shirt over his creased beige work pants asked, "What I gotta do to get a D out this class?"

I found it heartbreaking that the kid had such low expectations.

But when I told a veteran colleague and got a laugh, I knew I would be okay. He encouraged me to believe I could get through to that kid—and the rest of them. He said my chances would be better if I kept my sense of humor about it all.

Afternoon classes were quieter, sometimes much quieter; sometimes they would get so quiet that we could hear pigeons who had somehow nested inside a rusted-out air vent. One afternoon, a student named Cain started imitating those pigeons. A student named Abel told him to stop making fun of birds. Cain retorted that he was trying to communicate with them.

Cain fell asleep, and before I noticed and could try to rouse him, Abel snapped a combination lock inside the expander in Cain's earlobe. Cain woke up and demanded Abel open the thing that was pulling on his ear. Abel said he couldn't remember the combination. Eventually, I had to keep Cain and Abel from fighting. Really.

Stressed as I was—sweat soaking my shirt, heart racing—my appreciation for the absurdity of it all kept me from screaming or crying or just quietly giving up on myself and those kids.

It was like that a lot and for a while. Students testing me, pushing me—and each other. These kids, who'd never been successful in school, had long ago decided to mock the whole ordeal as if to prove it was the sham it felt like to them.

Jose and Carlos stand out in my memory of those early days—two massive guys who spent most of the class standing or wandering in the back of the room, probably because their girth made it uncomfortable for them to sit at the student chair-desks. They never did any work, no matter how much I encouraged or pleaded or threatened. They laughed at all my efforts, and when I would address the class, explaining things or trying to arouse a discussion, Jose or Carlos would raise a hand, and when I called on either of them, they would say, "You're doing a really good job, sir."

I didn't know what to make of it. They kept saying it every 20 or 30 minutes. At first, I assumed they were mocking me. On some level, they surely were. But it was so gentle and sounded so sincere, I couldn't help laughing—which probably encouraged them—and it wasn't until later in the year that I started thinking it was also an appreciation for not giving up on them and for laughing instead of losing my temper.

Where I needed a sense of humor the most, though, were my dealings with administrators and the Orwellian LA Unified School District. I still remember waiting for six hours in a hot and crowded district lobby to get processed as an employee and filling out forms, including one on which I had to pledge my allegiance to the country and against communism and another declaring that I had never abused a child (reassuring to know they so carefully vetted us). I remember the awful condition of the schools where I worked—crumbling buildings with unventilated freezing and sweltering classrooms, dim from broken lights, damp from leaky roofs, dank from mold seeping from the dirt foundation through floor holes where tiny eyes would sometimes peek up at us and kids would sometimes play whack-a-mole with their rolled-up notebooks. The classroom doors were eaten away by termites, broken windows covered with plywood. The totality of the degradation screamed inside of me whenever I discovered evidence of wasted money, which was everywhere.

Probably the most egregious example of the waste was on display in a massive office suite the district had leased, which lay empty except for one large room where district athletics sometimes held meetings. Looking for a working men's room one time, I found rooms being used as graveyards for broken office equipment, most of which were not very old. The criminal waste, coupled with all the neglect, was enraging. Nothing to laugh at—except that laughter was the only way to keep from screaming out loud about all the absurdities and obscenities

If I ever needed proof of how essential a sense of humor is, I just need to remember our school's first drama teacher. DJ was determined to get our students to do Shakespeare. None had previously had any meaningful experience reading or seeing or performing the Bard, but DJ's passion and dedication carried these kids to fully commit to the effort. He worked tirelessly to prepare them for the production, then, the night before the curtain was to rise, the guy playing Romeo was arrested in connection with a shooting he'd had nothing to do with—but which would keep him in juvenile detention for weeks. DJ never recovered from his frustration, and the rest of us watched him burn out and self-destruct, fighting with students and admins and compounding his misery.

I had great admiration for that drama teacher and I hope he's still in the teaching profession, and that he sometimes finds a way to laugh at the indignities, injustices, and frustrations.

When You Feel the Rage, Find a Way to Laugh

Don't expect the institutional outrages to get better. We should hope and, above all, try to push for sane policies and priorities and push against pettiness and corruption and hapless old stupidity, but we should manage our expectations and do whatever we can to keep our sense of humor intact.

When administrators refuse to find ways to pay for all the extra work I do and then dock me five minutes' pay because I got stuck behind an accident on the freeway coming to work, I try to find a way to soften my outrage by writing something obtuse or ironic or awkward in the "late sign-in" book as my "reason" for being late. I don't care if they ever read it, and I don't care how they react if they do. As long as I can amuse myself, I can quickly and painlessly put the petty nonsense behind me.

Back when our school languished in squalor, a few of my colleagues and I used to amuse ourselves by drawing comic strips about it during staff meetings or professional development. I wish we had phones with cameras in them back then. I would love to have saved that art, which, at the time, helped save my sanity.

Some of us used to hold detentions for, what one teacher referred to as, NBs and Gs ("naughty boys and girls"). We would assemble them in one of our rooms and blast music that was meant to be unpleasant for them—the playlist featured Lawrence Welk, Tiny Tim, "MacArthur Park" (the original and disco versions), opera from around the globe, and various post-modern polytonal offerings—while we would wear construction-worker earmuffs. I'm pretty sure it violated rules against corporal punishment, but the kids kind of enjoyed it and often asked for copies of the music (one year, seniors played "Bubbles in the Wine" and "The Chicken Polka" at their prom), so it was unclear whether it had much impact on student behavior (those detentions were always pretty full) but we had a lot of laughs, and so did most of the students.

I have been asked, more times than I can remember, to assist administrators in writing our accreditation reports—and by *assist*, I mean by pretty much writing the whole thing. The first time I was asked, I was still young enough to be outraged by the hypocrisy of painting over all of the school's deficiencies with no mention of everything that needed improving. I actually tried injecting some honesty into the document, but the principal read it closely and then fictionalized my confessions. One thing she didn't catch in her reading though—no one else did either—was the spine poem I created on the first page. It wasn't easy. I agonized over how to change the first letter of the first word on each line so that, if one read down the spine of the text, it spelled out THIS IS BS (I'm actually not even positive I abbreviated that last compound word). I don't believe that I would find it necessary to create a subversive spine poem on an accreditation report anymore, but at the time, it felt like a surreptitious protest that needed to be lodged—and the colleagues I told appreciated it.

Mostly, though, for me at least, it has always been about making the effort to see and laugh at all the ironies and absurdities. Like having a place on the campus labeled THE QUIET ZONE, which, of course, was the noisiest part of the school. Or walking into the principal's office one fall, when we had three unfilled teaching positions and fights breaking out all over the campus and finding her and one of her lieutenants brainstorming a mission statement for the school.

One spring morning, men wearing hazardous materials protective gear appeared on the roofs of our one-story bungalow classrooms. They told us they were conducting asbestos abatement. We asked if it was safe for us and our students to be there, and they shrugged. No one else would answer that question either. When we called the school district, they had no idea anyone was there.

One January, we returned from winter break to discover that a construction crew had piled dirt next to our campus, mountains of it dwarfing our bungalow classrooms. We could see it from almost every angle and sometimes smell it inside our rooms. Everything seemed dirtier. Some teachers said they were having trouble breathing. Enough parents complained that district officials came to the campus and spoke to everyone at an afterschool meeting. They assured us that it was, as they put it,

"Clean dirt." A few months later, 40-mile-an-hour Santa Ana winds blew through our campus, and my Advanced Placement Literature students got to experience a dust storm while they were reading *The Grapes of Wrath*. For an English teacher, it doesn't get any better than that.

Ditto for teaching irony to high school seniors taking English Composition in a Kindergarten room with the little coat hooks and cubbies and sinks and a playground through a backdoor that I let them play in at the end of class if they "were good."

I have even been able to laugh at the irony of professional development taught by facilitators who know less about teaching than the recipients of their "expertise" and students being able to make up a semester-long class in a day or two through district-approved online scams or any of the absurdities and obscenities of institutional corruptions that compromise what we try to do for students. It is all pretty infuriating and will, if we don't somehow laugh about it, grind away at the soul.

Find Colleagues You Can Laugh With

A sense of humor amid the stresses and outrages is far easier to maintain with colleagues who share that objective. The laughter tends to come more easily when it is shared. Multiple perspectives can help us laugh at all the confounding goofiness and the sublime stupidities that might otherwise—to paraphrase poet Charles Bukowski—slam our guts to pieces.

> A sense of humor amid the stresses and outrages is far easier to maintain with colleagues who share that objective.

It isn't only about the laughs, of course. Sometimes, just sharing a common understanding of the joys and miseries around us can be immensely reassuring. Sometimes, just having the right person to commiserate with can help us through all of it. I say the right person because I have found myself trying to commiserate with fellow educators who have expressed a kind of callousness and lack of general regard for our students. I do not find that at all helpful and, in fact, it troubles me.

It is the primary reason that I have spent almost no time eating lunch in faculty lunchrooms. In my experience, these are places that can permeate with bitterness and contempt. I cannot say whether that is always the case. There may be faculty dining places in which joy and positivity prevail. I just have not yet been in one that wasn't dominated by a lot of complaining without much irony or humor.

Even with irony and humor, I have always tried to minimize my own grievances and not make them a central element of the camaraderie forged with colleagues. The teachers with whom I've shared the most joy and laughter are the ones with whom conversations often veer away from work, and when they are about school, it is almost always an expression of our shared affection for our students. When it comes to the stress to which kids subject us, and we subject them and the dysfunction and inanity of the school, we keep it light.

And when we gossip and have some laughs at the expense of our colleagues, it is always with the utmost respect. Always. Of course.

It is always good to hear that a struggling teacher I am mentoring has colleagues with whom they can humorously commiserate. One recently told me about her fellow first-year teachers, abjectly overwhelmed, under-supported by anyone else on their campus, and trapped in a front-row seat to the tragic clown show that is the public education system's savagery toward the very children it is supposed to serve.

Still, they didn't realize how miserable they had seemed until their waitress at the bar where they drank together on Fridays after work wrote a note on their receipt in response to their generous tip. She wrote, "Thanks, Sad Teachers." After that, they started referring to each other as the sad teachers—and laughing more. And feeling less sad.

I have never had teacher drinking pals or done much after work hanging out with other teachers, but I have been extremely fortunate to always have at least one colleague with a sense of humor to help me keep mine. I hope you are at least as fortunate.

Laugh With the Students

Our students want to laugh. They need to laugh. Sometimes, they will do anything to laugh in order to rise above the agony of their mental stress and emotional turmoil. They will laugh at nonsense. They will laugh at each other, and they will generally jump at the chance to laugh at us. We might as well get used to that and try to laugh with them and enjoy it.

> Our students want to laugh. They need to laugh.

Kids love to pull pranks. They are a distraction from stresses and torments and can also be an ephemeral source of power. Kids pull them on each other and on us. It is always a good idea to be on guard and, as much as possible, to roll with it. I have had students ask me all the usual joke set-up questions with the juvenile and sometimes obscene punchlines—"Have you seen Boffa …? If your Uncle Jack was on the roof, would you help him off …?" and so on. I have had students hide things from me and snicker as I try to inconspicuously find them. They have tried to get me to eat very, very hot peppers that would probably turn me red and sweating—thankfully, that trick has thus far not worked—and students have managed to flip my backpack and once, when I had to step outside in an emergency, flipped my entire classroom, turning every piece of furniture upside down and facing the walls.

Students love to draw, especially unflattering or overly flattering portraits of us. I have been depicted in a Hawaiian skirt and in a Speedo and as a tented homeless person and a half-space alien. Also, as a body-builder and a basketball player, dunking my own head through the hoop. Mostly with an exaggerated jaw and/or eyebrows or just with an expression that suggests insanity.

I hang them up. All of them. Flattering and unflattering. To me, in a way, they are all flattering.

I let them draw on one of the whiteboards at the back of the classroom. Mostly, they make stick figures of their friend groups and spell out life advice and random poll questions about athletes, sports teams, and entertainers. Sometimes, they draw inappropriate things that I have to erase. I don't always see them in time. A few years ago, a student drew an upright dinosaur in pretty impressive detail, though I didn't really look all that closely at it or pay much attention to it, so I didn't notice when someone added a gang tattoo on its leg or when its toes were suddenly holding a gun or when someone constructed genitalia out of whiteboard magnets.

The principal didn't notice it either. Neither did his boss from the district office when they came to observe my class. Students and I had a good laugh about it after they left, and someone pointed out what we'd all missed.

Even in moments when we might feel urgency for things to be serious, it is often the case that if we concede to the joke, if we appreciate the joke—especially if it is at our expense—we can more easily get past it and get students to take us seriously.

Some students need to be funny—or try to be—and if we give them some space for that, we can earn their cooperation. If we show appreciation for their sense of humor, we can earn their loyalty. If we show appreciation for their sense of humor, we can earn their loyalty—and their love.

I am old now, and a little hard of hearing and sometimes forgetful, and I am bald—and kids can be pretty merciless in their ridicule. If I forget something, someone might cough out the word *senile*. They laugh at me spraying sunscreen on my head while heading outside for a fire or earthquake drill. I am glad they trust me enough to clown me to my face, and though I may sometimes feign irritation at the ridicule, I mostly laugh along.

When we can be good sports about being made fun of, we are teaching them a valuable lesson about maturity and the power of self-confidence. It isn't always easy to get there, though, especially as a young teacher, but I believe we can get there, all of us.

Years ago, some colleagues and I found ourselves consoling a first-year teacher who was having an emotional melt-down because a student had unrolled a condom over her stapler. I still remember her tearful lament, "They have no respect for me!"

My colleagues and I tried our best to keep from laughing—not at her sad state, not at all, but at the pitiful immaturity of putting a condom on the classroom stapler. Ultimately, though, we just couldn't hold it in. I felt terrible. I was afraid we were about to further humiliate and alienate this young teacher.

We really wanted to be supportive. All I could do was try to explain to her that the prank was just so dumb, so pathetic, such a typical immature boy thing, that we couldn't help laughing.

The young teacher seemed shocked by my explanation. I thought she was going to start crying harder and maybe run out of the room and maybe out of the school altogether. But instead, suddenly, she burst out laughing—still crying but now laughing too.

A few years later, she told me she couldn't get over how that stapler wearing a condom had gotten to her in the first place.

27

Change Is the Constant

In some pretty fundamental ways, public K–12 remains a fossil of the early 19th Century. Students in classrooms at tables or little desks, teachers teaching, passing judgment with letter grades, writing on a board, conforming to a bell schedule and a school calendar, and answering to a leadership structure modeled after a business or an army. Still, in many ways, the challenges of teaching effectively and thriving in this work are ever-changing.

I have seen and felt a lot change in 30-plus years, not the least of which is my own sensibility about this teaching thing. In the early days and weeks and years of it, when I endured the exhausting weight of inexperience and uncertainty, I impatiently awaited the moment when that ordeal would all be over, and I would achieve something resembling an equilibrium from which I would catch my breath and then coast. Turns out, though, that the equilibrium, if one can really call it that, was just a means by which to brace myself for all the earthquakes (metaphorical for most of you but also literal for my L.A. colleagues and me).

Change can come gradually or suddenly. Change can stir within our school, seep in from the community around us, or reach us from afar. Wherever and whatever its origins, I always try to remember that among the many roles of a teacher, none is more important than helping students understand and cope with what is happening around them and what is happening to them.

Kids Are and Aren't Like They Used to Be

Non-educator friends often ask me about the current condition of teenagers and whether I believe most of them will grow up to be productive adults. I am not sure they are asking the right person. All I can tell them is that most of the kids in my classes now have grown up in poverty in the shadow of gang violence. Like almost all kids of their generation, they have grown up online and experienced the isolation, uncertainties, and tragedies of the pandemic, but every other cohort of students I have taught has had challenges, too. I taught kids during the crack epidemic and the worst years of gang violence, teenage pregnancy, and mass incarceration that left many kids without one or both parents. My own generation seemed pretty hopeless in our own way at the time, so it doesn't take much imagination to realize that most of this current generation will probably somehow figure things out. I've already seen examples of it. I recently saw a student from three years ago. I can still remember her, as a senior, decrying the ineptitude of her peers and herself, saying that when they were adults, she would never go to a doctor her age or fly on a plane piloted by someone her age. But here she was, an adult in the world, confident and competent and seemingly with no memory of her previous lamentations.

I have found it useful to avoid generalizing too much about the students I teach, but it is worthwhile to observe and adjust to what I am seeing and hearing from them. I have observed that students in recent years seem more inward than students of ten or 20 or 30 years ago, though, of course, not nearly all of them.

There is much reporting among scholars and in the mass media about the current teenage mental health crisis, which teachers are witnessing firsthand. We are also observing radically changing attitudes from many of our students about anxiety and depression. Many students are now open about their own struggles, though there remain kids too proud—or ashamed—to admit they might benefit from any help. Often, these are the kids who need help the most, and we can help if we are willing to listen without judgment and offer our perspective while giving the space to act impervious to their traumas and tribulations. Sometimes, a student will only open up to a teacher because they feel the trust that comes with time and familiarity.

I saw an example of this just a few years ago when our school's softball team witnessed the beating and shooting of a man as they were boarding the bus to go to a game. Crisis counselors were brought in, but some students refused the help. One girl said things that disparaged anyone who did seek help for emotional or mental challenges. When I challenged her on that view, she ended up telling me about her own struggles with family dysfunction and toxic relationships. Soon, she was crying her eyes out and saying what a relief it was to talk about everything and ultimately opened up to the idea of talking to a trained professional.

I can say with confidence that more of my current students are comfortably and openly LGBTQ than they used to be and that when I began teaching, none of them were. I know this because dozens of former students from 20 or 30 years ago have told me they spent high school fearfully concealing who they were. I can also say that more students are accepting of diversity of all kinds, and so are teachers and other staff. I can recall when some teachers routinely expressed homophobia and did so with impunity. The culture and the mores of the school district have accommodated and supported and, in many ways, insisted upon this so that it is now the homophobes who are in the closet.

I wish this were true in every school or district or state, but I do suspect that levels of awareness and acceptance have elevated, at least somewhat, in most places, at least among students. I also know that such enlightenment is fragile. Tolerance and open-mindedness can be replaced by fear and bigotry; the future for many of our most vulnerable students is extremely uncertain, and if we care about them then we need to prepare them for that uncertainty. Some of us may be faced with difficult decisions about how far we are willing to go and how much we are willing to risk—including, potentially, our jobs—on their behalf. I remember back in 1994 when California passed Proposition 187, which would have denied public education to undocumented children, and educators all over the state were wrestling with whether to violate that law to protect their students. Ultimately,

187 was struck down by the courts, and no one ever had to act on or against it, but not before many of us had done a lot of soul-searching and understood in a much deeper way what it meant to be a teacher.

I have also seen positive change in the way that disabled students are treated. In recent years, I have taught an increasing number of students on the autism spectrum. These kids are far more knowledgeable and comfortable with who they are. And, for the most part, they enjoy far more acceptance and inclusion from their peers. Recently, our school's prom king was a young man with autism. He was also voted life of the party by the rest of the senior class for the yearbook superlative page.

The kids I teach seem to know more about the world than previous cohorts, the result, I suspect, of growing up online. They listen to music of all genres from all over the world and from the present and the past and are less likely to mock the old music I sometimes play in my classroom. There are still many gaps in their knowledge and a lot of misconceptions, and I suspect this is also the result of so much time on the internet and getting so much of their information through social media.

How does this impact teaching? I have made it a priority to help students develop more reliable ways to getting information, helping them understand how to vet sources of news and approach the web with sufficient skepticism. Beyond that, the realities of the digital universe and its influence on students influence my teaching in imperceptible ways. In my interactions with students. In how I talk to them, joke with them, and get serious with them. In how I encourage excellence and hold them accountable, and in how I encourage dissent and self-advocacy and reinforce their entitlement to be treated fairly and equitably.

Of course, I have also changed over the years, probably in more ways than I know. I am more patient with myself and with students. I thought I might get a little grouchy with age, but so far, the opposite has happened. I am careful not to say things that are inadvertently alienating to students—like referring to families as if they all have a mother and a father or referring to relationships as if only cis-gendered heterosexual people are in one. Some kids seem bemused by my insistence on the language of inclusion, and I do not begrudge them their bemusement. My job isn't to change their values; only to help them realize the values of the adult world, and especially the professional class of which most of them aspire to be a part. I try to be realistic about the degree to which social media and other digital activities reduce the time many students spend and the interest level they have in reading or writing, and how antiquated those passions might seem to them, but I won't ever stop promoting the beauty of language, the wonders of storytelling, and the magic of a great book.

I try, in every way I can, to help students adjust to everything that is changing around them, and I try to keep changing myself, responding to changes in the school and especially in the students, finding better ways to accommodate and appreciate all of them.

It Is a Different World All the Time

The external influences on students and educators are ever-changing, the pressures sometimes increasing, and a clear understanding of them often elusive.

The communities of which our schools are a part can have a substantial impact on the culture and ethos of the institution. Local tensions between adults can morph into antipathy among students. I have seen and dealt with this many times in many ways over the years in a community that has undergone radical demographic changes, political upheavals, waves of drug and crime epidemics, a proliferation—in the neighborhood and throughout the region—of unhoused people, some scattered gentrification, and the devastation of many low-income neighborhoods during the first year of the Covid-19 pandemic.

> Helping students understand and respond to the changes around them is an important part of what we can do for them.

Helping students understand and respond to the changes around them is an important part of what we can do for them. So is helping them understand all the reasons for these shake-ups, small and big, and the ways in which they reflect the influences of local politics, including school board elections, and all the public pressures and legalities constraining schools and school districts, and all the decisions that impact kids without always taking their best interests into consideration.

We need to be ready to roll with all the punches thrown at us by the ever-changing circumstances in which we are teaching. Leadership changes in our school and district can be destabilizing. I have seen more than one new principal or superintendent declaring some version of "It's a new day"—words that should be inspiring but, to those of us who have been around, are mostly ominous. I try to stay positive and hope for the best, and have managed to navigate and make the best of even the most unpleasant and oppressive reforms.

Just be ready. Don't get complacent, and always remember the goal—helping kids. Whatever we can do, whatever the situation.

Technological Grips

When I began teaching, technology in the classroom was a phone on the wall (if you had one) and the bells that chimed to begin and end classes (if you had them). In the strictest sense, also the pens and pencils with which students wrote, the binding that held together the books that students read, and the grade book I carried around and locked away from students.

Today, we take attendance on computers or tablets or phones through a (hopefully) secure internet connection. We assign work and grade it on digital devices and communicate with students and admins and colleagues through servers and platforms accessible all over the United States. Like most working professionals, we get buried in emails and other messages. We also send urgent communications that sometimes get ignored. Ambitious—and sometimes desperate—teachers network with teachers throughout the country and the world, sharing advice and lessons.

Mostly, technology and the internet work, but glitches and shutdowns can be immensely aggravating and eat up time none of us have. In the district in which I teach, when a counselor moves a student from one class to another, the grades from the old class disappear, usually before the teacher can screenshot or otherwise keep track of them. And attendance for that day no longer reads "submitted," though there is no notification that the teacher now appears, unjustifiably, to be delinquent.

Most onerous of all, perhaps, is the somewhat Orwellian aspect of this 21st-century way of doing things. We ought not mind that admins anywhere can look at our attendance or electronic grade book or, like everywhere else, our work Email, but the ability to perpetually scrutinize can create an overbearing style of leadership that values abstract data collections, easily graphed and charter while ignoring the more important nuances of teaching and learning. Quality of teaching must be observed for a sustained time, not gleaned from a computer dashboard.

Depending on who you talk to, the Covid-19 crisis showed us the value of digital devices and the internet in keeping school going despite the once-in-a-century pandemic, or it enabled us to more easily isolate kids from their teachers and each other. One thing we discovered is that a computer screen and even a secure connection—and most of my students did not have reliable internet—is no substitute for a caring and engaging teacher in the same room.

And, yet, since the return to campuses, online education has continued to proliferate, replacing in-person learning experiences. These alternatives have helped raise graduation rates and lower the number of dropouts, but often at the expense of serious scholarship and real student engagement. There are fully automated online classes that AI can, and often does, take for the student.

Not all children are using these opportunities to scam the system. For some kids, these electronic classes represent a legitimate way to learn without all the distractions and drama of a classroom and a way to make up classes without having to travel through dangerous neighborhoods to adult school in the late afternoon.

For teachers, online meetings and training can be a welcome alternative to the ordeal of getting to some other location after work—though many among us are more than tired of the 2D tedium and the reminder of those grim days of the pandemic.

Teachers should be prepared for more tech revolutions invading and, in some cases, enhancing our classrooms. Perhaps the best preparation is an open mind and an openness to change. Resist the belief that success can be replicated in identical fashion year after year. If we remain reflective and improvement-oriented in our teaching, we are less likely to be blindsided by external change.

I remember how many colleagues and admins were unprepared for the computerization of the schools—luddite educators retreating and retiring or just stressing out and complaining.

We may now believe the revolution is essentially over. Digital tech and the internet have made their mark and insinuated themselves, and nothing much will fundamentally change in the future. I believe we would be foolish to make that assumption. I have no idea what things will be like in ten or twenty years and I doubt anyone else does, either.

Hopefully, we will do a better job of harnessing the next generation of technological innovation and with human intelligence guiding decisions. Thus far, the positive effects of technology on the classroom have been largely offset by the negative, not the least of which is the profound and massive distraction it has created and the proliferation of opportunities for students to sabotage their own learning through dubious shortcuts and blatant cheating. Coping with that is the subject of this book's next chapter.

28

Teaching through the Learning Tools of Evasion and Distraction

When I began teaching in the late 20th century, I wondered how I was supposed to compete for student attention with television and movies and the rest of the popular culture, which seemed to have kidnapped and strangled their imaginations and sensibilities. Now, the movies and television, along with video games, an endless jukebox, and the teenage social centers are in their pockets—or in their hands and in their gaze.

How is any teacher supposed to compete for attention with all that?

Schools and districts are trying to keep students off their phones during the school day with a variety of policies, none of them perfect, all of them subject to outrage, pushback, and sabotage.

Meanwhile, artificial intelligence (AI) and other digital innovations have made shortcutting and outright cheating easier, and so we find ourselves in a technological war with students for the sake of their learning, trying to keep one step ahead of them with tools that detect and discourage plagiarism—and only sometimes falsely accuse students of academic fraud.

These are battles worth waging, but I have never been interested in making them the focus of my response to these electronic impediments to learning. I don't suggest you do either. The power of these digital tools has implications far beyond what

DOI: 10.4324/9781003538936-33

students are and are not doing in my classes. They are a pervasive influence on us all, and their influence on students ought to compel us to help them learn how to navigate the future in this brave new world.

Coaxing Kids (and Ourselves) toward Responsible Use: Phones

I know few people of any age who haven't at some time found themselves wasting hours staring at the small screen suspended in their palm, scrolling toward the end of time, or sitting among live human beings engaged instead with an exchange of text bubbles with someone somewhere else.

If you are one of the lucky or strong few who have managed to disdain all digital vices—and good for you—then you, better than anyone, can help students find their way to conquering this scourge and reigning in the outsized place phones now have in most kids' lives.

If, like me, you are only slightly better than most students in your self-control with a personal computing device, then let your empathy and wisdom and your own desire for self-improvement lead them to a more sane and reasonable relationship with the phones. Educators often follow the impulse to get rid of phones during school altogether. A substantial amount of research supports this approach, and if a school can manage the complicated logistics of getting phones out of the hands of their students, those students are surely better off. But students don't spend all their waking hours in class. Being conscious and reflective, aware, and smart about their relationship to their phones is an essential life skill for pretty much anyone coming of age now.

Social media accessed by young people on these and other devices are a hub of bullying, social alienation, and sleep deprivation, especially when coupled with gaming—which has now morphed into its own version of social media. The physical and mental health effects can devastate kids, especially the most vulnerable. I have had students recount to me, in discussions and writing, some disturbing experiences going down internet rabbit holes, retreating into digital caves, or being threatened, harassed, and humiliated by peers and strangers or being groomed and even stalked by internet predators.

How we—the grown-ups—have allowed our children to be exposed to such harm is kind of shameful, and there is, it seems, far too much money being made at their expense to ever expect those with power and position to do anything meaningful about it. That leaves willing teachers and parents to help kids develop reasonable and healthy approaches to the pixelated online universe.

I lead with my own struggle, helping students to understand how I win and lose the battle of using my devices without giving in to their seduction. Giving in does not constitute moral failure. We are targets of sophisticated programming, algorithms designed to suck our eyeballs and our minds into the dot-com universe. There are articles and documentaries that are worth sharing with students. Help them understand what we are all up against, our individual and collective vulnerabilities, and how we are targeted. When we avoid judgment, kids are more likely to listen. When we help kids understand their challenges, they are more likely to want to overcome them.

> Help them understand what we are all up against, our individual and collective vulnerabilities, and how we are targeted. When we avoid judgment, kids are more likely to listen. When we help kids understand their challenges, they are more likely to want to overcome them.

I work in a school district and state that have mandated phone restrictions in K–12 schools beginning in the coming year, and I welcome the effort, and however successful it is, I will continue my effort to help kids educate themselves about the power and perils of their phones. I will be open with them about my own struggles to limit phone use, especially the time-wasting variety.

I will share my experience experimenting with periodic e-detoxing, sleeping with my phone charging in a different room. I will caution them about phone etiquette in the adult world, especially for those in the professional class to which most of my students aspire—about where and under which circumstances they will be expected to have their phones silenced and about the social and professional consequences of obnoxious public phone use.

A recent assignment I tried with a summer school class of heavily phone-addicted students was to have them spend an hour writing descriptions of their scroll—everything they watched or did on their phone, in detail. Most found the assignment annoying since it slowed them down and forced them to confront the vapidness, killing the fun. It also helped some of them realize what a visual narcotic they were hooked on. I do not believe any of them radically altered their relationship with these devices immediately after, but I think it is reasonable to hope that, in the long run, the experience might help influence them to be smarter with their smartphones.

Coaxing Kids (and Ourselves) toward Responsible Use: Artificial Intelligence

In my midnight of the soul moments, I sometimes wonder if we aren't careening toward a hallucinatory existence in which AI creates the lesson for us, then completes the assignment for students, then grades it while we all sit around scrolling into oblivion.

Actually, most teachers find it acceptable to use AI as a shortcut to performing our job, and an increasing number of us accept AI as a useful tool for students, but it is a perilous one, easily tempting kids to let it do things for them.

Arming ourselves with software tools to catch AI and other cheating methods is a reasonable response for teachers and a good start. False positive error rates for these programs are very low. They are not, however, zero—and we ought not to be comfortable with any possibility of falsely accusing any student of cheating. Ever. A positive diagnosis ought not be an automatic indictment but a conversation starter. I often find that my own eyes and analysis are sufficient AI detectors to ask a student to explain their ideas, their diction, and other rhetorical choices.

Such questioning often leads to confessions or half-confessions, which are opportunities for me to reinforce the importance of original work. Not just for the sake of academic integrity—a lot of kids don't care much about that—but to ensure authenticity and the power of personal expression and the desire to be smart and well-prepared for success. We are better off avoiding the game of academic cops and robbers and focusing instead on compelling students to want to be original and aspire to be brilliant.

I do not find this a difficult argument to make. The ability to write is an essential academic and life skill. There may be many situations in which using AI to write a memo or short informative Email is entirely appropriate, but there will inevitably be times when our students will need to convey what is in their hearts and having to rely on a machine to try and do that for them is beyond pathetic.

I have conveyed to students a number of my own high-stakes writing challenges and how grateful I was that I had the ability to be successful. Like writing a letter to a college business office about an impoverished student they had dropped for failing to show up for an orientation she had no way to get to and no money to pay for. My letter was a pretty strong indictment of a university system that boasted its success in serving first-generation economically disadvantaged college students, willing to reject one of its most disadvantaged students because of her extreme poverty but the letter also left room for some kind soul reading it to be the hero. It got that student reinstated and the admissions directors who'd read it promised to look after her thereafter.

Or the appeal I wrote to the California Interscholastic Athletics office on behalf of the basketball team I coached after opposing players attacked our guys, and their school tried to blame the altercation on us and get our team banned from playoffs; none of our players were suspended, and we went on to win a city championship. Or the letter I wrote to a jailhouse warden on behalf of a former student who was imprisoned awaiting trial and not being treated for a serious illness; within a few days, he was transported to the hospital and treated.

I ask students if any of them would ever want to leave such urgent matters to an AI program. I ask if they believe that any binary machine, however powerful, even with extraordinarily sophisticated software, can produce authentic passion and humanity born out of the human experience it does not and cannot have. Mostly, kids are in agreement that such a presumption is absurd and obscene.

I am not delusional. I know how tempting those electronic shortcuts are to some students when they are tired or have surrendered to any of the many more fun things to do or just don't feel like it. I don't ever expect to change all their minds all the time. My goal for cheaters and potential cheaters is to get them to start believing in themselves. Not just that they can learn to write well but that they have something unique to say and that is worth saying. That their experience and perspective are important. And that writing isn't merely a tool of expression. It is self-exploration. It is a powerful way for us to get to know ourselves, a way for us to become fully human.

And it is a means by which we can make ourselves smarter. Writing is thinking in action. Writing helps us reflect on and refine our thinking. Writing is a way for us to find ourselves intellectually, a way to develop and strengthen our voice. Articulating ourselves in writing makes us more comfortable and confident and effective in our verbal expression. AI cannot speak for us—not, at least, in most situations—but our pens (or keyboards) and our tongues and our minds are all connected, and we ought not to short-circuit those connections.

> That is my pitch to students—over and over.
> In the hope that it somehow, eventually sticks.
> Feel free to borrow as much of that as you see fit.

29

Sanity First, Martyrdom Is Overrated

The perils of burnout will probably always be with us, even for teachers with confidence and credibility. There is always more—*much more*—we can do for our students, and there is often more that our admins want us to do.

Do not ever assume that anyone will look out for your wellbeing. Kids are selfish by nature. They are built to use us up. Administrators are programmed to exploit and badger us, and not all of them are smart or strong enough to resist that programming. We are expected to look out for ourselves, and we've got to do that, for our own sake and the sake of our students.

Some teachers seem to understand that from day one. As deeply as they care about students and want to be great teachers, they have no intention of sacrificing themselves in the process. No one ought to ever expect any teacher to do that.

Even teachers who enter the profession wanting to go above and beyond to make a difference in the lives of kids should always remember that we are no good to them if we burn out and that if we ignore our own needs—for rest and peace of mind, for a healthy balance of friends and family and work—we may not be able to sustain ourselves for long. If it is our goal to make this a career and to

> We are no good to them if we burn out and if we ignore our own needs.

make a difference for kids, then nothing is more important for us or our students than that sustainability, now and in the future.

That Work-Life Balance Thingy

When I hear songs from the early 90s, I am always flooded with memories of those first days, weeks, and months as a full-time teacher, and what I remember most is that feeling that I belonged, that I had a purpose much bigger than my own natural selfishness. Those kids needed so urgently to learn, to gain skills and knowledge—many despite themselves—and they also needed adults to care about them and listen to them, guide them and warn them. And drive them home sometimes because someone on the streets was looking to hurt them or take them to county jail to visit their brother or their uncle who was like a father and then help them through their sadness and their fear of what was going to become of them.

Giving myself over to the mission of helping these kids was both terrifying and gratifying. It filled me with a sense of purpose and vanquished most of the youthful insecurities that had dogged me. It also threatened to consume me and burn me out.

I wish I could claim to have been smart enough to see that and place some limits on the time and energy I would devote, money I would spend (despite how pathetic that starting salary was), and risks I would take on behalf of kids; the truth is that it wasn't until my marriage began to fall apart that I began to reconsider the give and take of my role as a teacher, coach, and mentor.

So, I might be the wrong person to tell anyone else anything about balance, but I have learned the hard way that the needs of students are never-ending. Their unrealized potential as students and as people and our unrealized potential to help them, the totality of the whole endeavor is perpetually overwhelming.

It can humble us. And it can crush us.

Words that helped steer me toward a more sustainable perspective came to me one morning when I had a class of 11th graders reading Raymond Carver's "Cathedral," a remarkable short story about a physically blind man who teaches an emotionally and spiritually blind man to see with his heart. At one point, the emotionally blind man is watching TV, as if to mock the physically blind man whose response is humorous and open-hearted, and ultimately the TV-watching man begins to try to help the other understand what he is looking at—a documentary about cathedrals. During that scene, the physically blind man recites everything he knows about cathedrals, including this about the people who built them: "The men who began their life's work on them, they never lived to see the completion of their work. In that wise, bub, they're no different from the rest of us, right?"

Being a teacher means being part of a project that is massively bigger than we are. Nothing we do will ever be enough, and so everything we do has to be enough. We have to find a way to be okay with falling short or we will torment ourselves and ultimately render ourselves useless to our students.

> Being a teacher means being part of a project that is massively bigger than we are.

The world is a lousy place for a lot of people and helping tip the balance, however slight, toward something better is always worthwhile. So is taking care of our own needs and having a joyous personal and family life.

It is wrong to be indifferent to the world's suffering and injustices. It is equally wrong to ignore our own needs.

There is no respect without self-respect.

There is no love without self-love.

Avoiding the Martyrdom Trap

Tragically, unsettlingly, I feel compelled to say that in modern teaching there is literal martyrdom. Teachers have died shielding students from barrages of bullets ripping through hallways and classrooms. Active shooter drills are a regular routine for most teachers, while we hope we don't ever have to die saving a student—but meanwhile make the calculation in our minds. The regularity of children and teenagers gunned down at school is so awful that little attention gets paid to the slaughtered teachers who die at rates disproportionate to their students. As it should be, right? Except that none of this should be, and the fact that some teachers have had to be heroes is just the most grotesque manifestation of the exploitation to which self-sacrificing people are regularly subjected.

As a first year teacher, I was impressed by my veteran colleagues who were self-styled crusaders for the mission of saving kids. Like Moses Robinson who had survived multiple tours in Vietnam and was determined now to steer young black men away from gangs and self-destruction and toward a political awakening and a college education. Or Roger Butcher who had spent more than a decade with the Peace Corps helping people in rural India and elsewhere aspire to economic sustainability and was now trying to apply those principles of self-reliance to disaffected kids living in poverty in the aftermath of the L.A. civil unrest. It was a little intoxicating to find myself collaborating with those and other missionary educators.

I remember looking at my first paycheck, feeling the insult of it, and then telling myself it didn't matter because we were accomplishing so much with at least some of these kids. It didn't matter because it didn't seem to matter to most of my colleagues because they were willing to suffer for the sake of the kids.

I also remember the praise I got from the principal and some of her bosses. The smiles and admiration for staying late to help kids, tutoring through my lunch, helping seniors write essays to get into college until well into the evening, chaperoning weekend field trips, and never asking to be paid for any of it. And why would I worry about money when I was immersed in the lives of kids whose poverty kept trying to defeat them in every possible way?

There was a skeptic on the staff. Maybe more than one, but Kevin Kennedy was the one willing to express it. I do not believe he cared any less about the kids than Moses or Roger, and I thought Kevin was a particularly effective teacher. But he wasn't buying the monastic martyrdom thing. He would caution everyone about how much we were all being asked to do beyond our professional responsibilities. He wouldn't exactly say it as a complaint.

His argument was pragmatic. He cited his church to illustrate. He said people always volunteered to do things, but they couldn't always be relied upon. He said people get tired of doing things when their time is being taken for granted. He said that for the sake of our students, we ought to be paid for our time.

I don't know how much his argument resonated with anyone. Nothing much changed. I do not know if the principal was willfully withholding what she knew she could have paid us or if she just didn't know any better. Budgets and financial management were not her strong suit, but I have seen other administrators boast about the dedication of teachers at their school and how they go the extra mile for students and I have come to understand that is code for getting teachers to work extra for nothing. I remain fond of my first principal, who hired me and encouraged me, but when she retired, her successor saw what some of us were doing for students, how much time and energy we were devoting to the cause and figured out how to pay us for the effort.

The difference Pam Jackson made was profound. Our school became a much better place in which to work, and that made it an even better place to learn. She made teachers feel appreciated and respected, and we worked even harder for her (she also went hard at the few teachers who weren't doing right by our students, but that is another matter).

Jackson spoiled my colleagues and me, and I am still spoiled. My time is worth as much as any other person and money always equals respect. The system seems, at least for the moment, designed to devalue the work we do. Plenty of lip service to our essential role in the lives of the children for whom the schools are built and staffed and otherwise funded. And yet, we find ourselves too often having to remind people who have far less direct impact on students that our time and talent and energy have value.

The system, in fact, often pays people inversely according to how much their work impacts students—a flagrant devaluing of the very students whose learning and well-being is supposed to be our priority.

We ought not accept this. For the sake of students, we should always demand the respect that teachers and students deserve.

30

Don't Let Heartbreak Bury You

For all the small student annoyances and the steady flow of administrative outrages—and the chronic exhaustion—my teaching experience has been overwhelmingly joyful.

The celebrations come often. Not just those monumental accomplishments I get to share with students—first in family graduations, college acceptance, college graduation, etc. The small affirmations are nearly constant—a student's breakthrough in understanding, a sudden leap in skill, an intensified academic interest as well as student acts of kindness and spasms of maturity and outright emotional, intellectual, and behavioral transformations.

I am profoundly grateful that those joys have far outweighed all the disappointments, failures, and tragedies because even in that equation, the heartbreaks can sometimes be devastating.

Sadness, to varying degrees has always been a part of the job. Working through it without becoming numb to it has been one of my greatest challenges. I don't know how talented or skilled I am at this emotional endurance. I would defer to firemen, paramedics, police, healthcare professionals, and combat soldiers who all have immensely more to cope with.

What I can tell you is that we are not immune, especially because we work with kids and because if we are lucky and we are effective, they will get emotionally attached to us—and we will become emotionally invested in them.

Small and Not-So-Small Things

As soon as I became competent enough to see kids as individuals—not just the chaotic mass I had to try to contain—I was immediately struck by the small bits of sadness: kids isolated by peers, emotionally neglected by family, unheard and unseen, frustrated and alienated, terrified and depressed and too proud to admit it. Or just going through it, enduring hardships that can compound for teenagers.

You see it far too much. A lonely kid spends nutrition or lunch break sitting alone on the stairs or the hallway floor. Another kid wanders in a remote part of campus crying because it's the anniversary of her mother's passing. I read student papers and college application essays that make casual mention of parents taken by cancer or dying by suicide or murdered in the street or deported suddenly without ever saying goodbye. Kids abused by their parents or other relatives, then ostracized by their family for reporting it. Or kids who feel unloved and misunderstood and misplaced in the world.

Mostly, these pieces of pathos are not overwhelmingly difficult to endure. Often, they are opportunities to help students. By listening, sympathizing, and maybe adding a little perspective. Sometimes all a student needs is to have their pain recognized and to be given some credit for enduring it. As awful as it is to see a young person suffer, it is equally inspiring to see them gather the courage and strength to rise of above their hardship.

> Sometimes all a student needs is to have their pain recognized and to be given some credit for enduring it.

Sometimes, their challenges challenge us. A great student, about to change the family story, gets pregnant and gives up her goals. Another great student gets a scholarship to an elite college, but her diabetic parents convince her to stay and take care of them. A parent won't provide financial documents a student needs to get financial aid for college. I have, at times, tried to help kids solve these dilemmas, but mostly, I can only hope and encourage and mostly it feels insufficient.

Or a kid with severe migraine or sickle cell disease is gone from school for weeks at a time, trying to keep up with our class and soldier through the physical and emotional agonies of their disjointed life. It can mean a lot to them that we understand their challenges, but it often feels pretty feeble. I suppose humility is our best approach. We cannot fix everything our students need fixed, but it can be difficult not to feel like that is a copout.

For many teachers, the full inclusion of special education students is as humbling as it gets, a full-on confrontation with our limitations. Having profoundly disabled children in our classrooms can be an opportunity to enrich their lives as well as the lives of our mainstream students and teach tolerance and empathy.

It is also just really sad. My most profound experience of this happened when I was doing extra hours as a supplemental homeschool teacher for the school district, driving to the homes of kids too sick or injured to attend school in person. Kids with cancer. Kids paralyzed from gunshots or living with crippling illnesses. It reminded me, at times, of visiting my late brother when he was living at Unit 88 of Camarillo State Hospital and Developmental Center and being overwhelmed by the terrible what-ifs, not just his but all the other people whose lives were so profoundly narrowed by fate and whose families were devastated by the tragedy. I am always happy to see that full inclusion has opened up the lives of such children, even if only a little, and I am glad that it still moves me, sometimes to tears, to see children who've been dealt such an unfair hand and who somehow muster the courage and strength to keep going.

I know it has made me a better teacher. I like to think I have endured all this sorrow without paying too big an emotional price. I consider myself a happy and relaxed person, but sometimes people ask me what's wrong when I don't think anything is wrong and then I wonder. I try to smile as much as I can—so that I won't hear such questions but also because it reminds me of every reason I have to be joyful for myself and my family, and for most of my students and former students.

We cannot remind ourselves enough of our joys; we cannot smile too much.

The Unthinkable

Over the years, I have become accustomed to a lot of the sadness that comes with teaching kids. Still, I refuse to ever prepare myself for the death of a student.

With 200 students to worry about each year—and contact with many of them after graduation—deaths may be a statistical inevitability, but I have no plans to surrender to that idea. And I don't think anyone ever should. Every student of ours is precious (however annoying they can be) and every loss is unacceptable.

And yet, it does happen. It has happened to my students and former students and to those of every other teacher I know.

It happened during my first year as a teacher. A young man shot to death in the street. And that kept on happening, at least once every year or two. Illness and car accidents also took the lives of students and former students. Mostly, my colleagues and I were too busy consoling our surviving students—which sometimes included their siblings—to have much time for our own sorrow.

But then there were moments when it would just hit me, when it would add up and pile on and I'd feel the weight of all the grief—mine and the kids and the parents who'd had to bury their kids. I haven't always known what to do with all that grief other than turn it to outrage and try to turn it into some kind of action. Be a better teacher, mentor the troubled kids a little harder, honor the memory of these kids and what they might have become through my own hard work, and by yelling a little louder at all the forces within the school and the school system making it harder on teachers and students.

I've never known what to say to the parents, some of whom I've gotten to know pretty well trying to figure what to do with their kid while they are alive and while we are all believing there was a long future to worry about. I am always deeply humbled—and, as a parent myself, terrified—by their bottomless grief. I have never shied away from entering the orbit of their agony, and I believe that has helped me endure my own very small part of it.

I believe it has also helped me always remain empathetic with all parents and always remember how much is beyond their control. More than anything, these awful moments have helped me to maintain the ability to always see and feel and say something good about a kid, and to remember to say something nice to them, however unkind they might be toward me or anyone else.

The most agonizing lessons are the ones learned when a student or former student dies by suicide. I worked for a principal years ago who shared her greatest regret as an educator. It happened when she was a teacher. A student came to talk to her after school on a Friday afternoon. She asked the student if it was important, and the student said no and they agreed to talk on Monday morning—and the kid died by suicide over the weekend. How was my former principal supposed to know? I didn't think she should let that tragedy haunt her. But of course, her story has haunted me for more than 30 years—and I have never let a student convince me that what they were feeling or what they needed to talk about wasn't important.

Even the former students, years removed from my classroom—sometimes having experienced military combat and all the traumas of that—when I hear that they've ended their own lives, I cannot help wondering if there was anything, five or ten or 20 years ago that I might have been able to say or do for them.

Stupid, I know. Crazy. Most of all grandiose. Which I'm afraid goes with the territory. Thinking we can help all these kids. Sometimes, that is the only alternative to giving up.

Enduring Disappointment

Somewhere in all this is just the right balance of second-guessing ourselves without letting the failures defeat us. It is the cycle of self-reflection and improvement. Fleeting satisfaction to stave off the dreaded complacency.

It happens often, mostly in manageable ways. Kids fail my class and I wonder if I could have done more to motivate them. Or they've messed up and gotten kicked out of school or been lost to the streets, and I wonder if there was something more I could have done to intervene. I am sure that I have an outsized sense of responsibility about that (there's that grandiosity again).

Years ago, I let a young man make up most of a class in a few last-minute assignments so that he could graduate. A few years later, he was incarcerated and though I knew there were many factors contributing to his downfall, and though he has long since taken full responsibility for everything he's done and has now served his time and put his life back together, I do still wonder if things might have been different if I'd held him more accountable when he was my student.

Needless to say, we cannot control what our students do when they are not with us—we can only hope to influence their behavior when they are in our presence. But the more we care about them, the more vulnerable we are when things go wrong and dreams are deferred.

I believe that is a burden worth enduring.

But I also believe that such burdens are entirely up to us. We do not owe anyone our agony or angst. We are paid to be teachers and it is up to us to decide what, beyond the legal requirements, are the obligations of that job. We are teachers, and anything we give beyond that is our gift. For me, those gifts have come back to me with exponential interest.

31

Give and Get Support

There is power in collaborating with those who share our goals and in recognizing the limits of individual success. Collectively, we can accomplish so much more.

Teaching can be lonely work, especially the first weeks, months, and years on the job. It takes time, for most of us, to adapt to the constant company of kids and to feel as if those kids are partners with us in their learning. When things don't go well, for a minute or an hour or a whole school day, we can feel isolation in our frustration and angst.

Schools are not always friendly or welcoming to new teachers and when we are anxious and stressed, the indifference can feel like outright hostility. I hope that is never your experience, but for too many new teachers it is. Don't take it personally. The stress of the job doesn't always bring out the best in everyone.

Find support somewhere. If not in your building, then elsewhere. A social media teacher community, perhaps—there are many. Track me down and send an Email if you have to. There is always support out there—people who understand the vital importance of helping new teachers become a force in the lives of kids.

Create Your Supports

By the end of my first week as a student teacher, I was a mess. It wasn't just how lame I felt trying to get through to the kids. I was drowning in student papers—and didn't even have a full load of classes. I felt terminally frazzled. Then, after the bell mercifully ended my last Friday class, a student peeked into the classroom and asked if I needed a teacher's assistant.

I thought her showing up at that moment was divine intervention and told her so. She probably thought I was out of my mind, and perhaps I was, and probably she'd seen her share of teachers who were.

As any experienced teacher knows, most high school TAs just want a free period to come late and chill, maybe do a little homework, sleep if they can get away with it. Occasionally, I could get her to pass out or collect papers, and she accompanied a few ailing kids to the nurse's office. Otherwise, she tended to create more work for me than she helped with.

But the following year, when I became a full-time teacher at a different school, I discovered that the math teachers had a little hustle going. They would convince their best students to TA for them, correcting homework and tests, entering grades, and pretty much relieving them of nearly all their paperwork!

I never tried to replicate their hack—English tests aren't multiple choice (not mine, anyway) and there really aren't any simple answer keys—but the more valuable lesson was in always looking for and figuring out ways to get help and reduce the impossible burdens of our job.

I found other colleagues willing to share their best practices, including ways to be more efficient and less frazzled, like marking papers in a systematic way, looking for and critiquing specific things and not trying to point out everything at once. I met teachers from other schools—at district trainings and other official events—and exchanged contact info and leaned on some of them when I could and let them lean on me when I could help.

Some of you may be lucky enough to find yourself at a school with a support system in place for new and struggling teachers or enough gracious colleagues to welcome you and help you get acclimated. A teacher I mentored recently was one of many new teachers hired the same year, and what they were all able to offer each other was mutual sympathy and a place in which to commiserate while they figured it all out.

If you are fortunate enough to be in such circumstances, get the most out of it, and if you have to, be the one who initiates the camaraderie. Start the group chat and organize the once or twice a week lunches together, find a bar or someplace to meet after work on Fridays.

As new teachers, you may not feel that you have much to offer each other, but multiple perspectives are almost always better than one weary mind. Nothing was more difficult for me back then than finding ways to identify success—mine and the students. Without that, it was easy to become demoralized. Having contact with colleagues—however new they were—talking, encouraging, complaining—whatever—helped me better realize what I was doing right and gave me hope that I had something to offer.

At the very least, colleagues can always provide each other with empathy and some laughs, and as everyone grows and learns, from successes and from failures, there are endless insights to share. No one has all the answers, but together we can figure a lot out.

> Just as believing in our students can keep them going through the worst moments of their lives, believing in each other can ensure that we are available and strong for those kids.

Just as believing in our students can keep them going through the worst moments of their lives, believing in each other can ensure that we are available and strong for those kids.

Be Nice to the Subs—and Everyone Else

Sometimes the best move we can make for our own well-being is to be friendly and open with our colleagues, even those who seem indifferent or even hostile toward us.

Most teachers I have found to be relatively nice people, but the pressures and outrages and humiliations of the work can turn us defensive, sullen, and even oddly territorial. That feeling can be contagious. But we can transcend whatever foul mood is permeating inside the building if we can manage to always assume the best of everyone. Collegiality can be equally contagious, and even if colleagues are slow to respond to it, making positive gestures can help maintain a good mood toward our work and our students.

New teachers ought not be expected to take the lead with positive vibes, but we are better off being willing to when necessary. Sometimes, the best way to get the support of our colleagues is to offer our support, in whatever way we can.

For me, that began with reaching out to the substitutes that came through my school. I had once been a sub and remembered how lonely that could be so whenever I saw one in the office or in the hallway, I always introduced myself and, if they hadn't been given a key—which was often the case—offered to let them into the restroom.

Most were very appreciative, and I think that witnessing my graciousness made a few of the wary veteran teachers see me in a different light, but most valuable for me was how it made me feel like I belonged.

It also, somehow, helped me feel entitled to ask others for help when I needed it.

Don't Ever Be Afraid to Ask for Help

Teacher pride is real. It is also quite understandable. Most of us have moments of embarrassment and even humiliation—even if only we realized it. The isolated nature of the work can leave us thinking that every other teacher in the building is delivering an instructional masterpiece every class period.

This can render us too self-conscious to ask anyone for help or guidance.

Teachers—like most other people—can be competitive. We want to be the best. We can even be jealous when students rave about another teacher. This is ridiculous, of course. We want our students to be successful. We want them to enjoy the benefits of great teaching. But we are human, and sometimes we have to make ourselves make the effort to overcome our insecurities.

One effective way to become a great teacher is to learn from great teachers—and we ought to trust our students to know who they are. One quality I believe all great teachers have in common is humility and enough trust to ask someone for help. Another quality is a willingness to humbly share strengths and wisdom and to be open about how we might need to improve. Also, an ability to always keep our shortcomings in perspective.

We are not burdening our colleagues by asking for help. Not the good ones, anyway. Always, please, remember that.

I am constantly telling students that when they ask me for help, they are helping me do my job (and when they are afraid to ask for help, they make my job much harder).

The same is true between colleagues.

Supporting one another goes both ways—asking for help is as helpful as providing it, and helping each other help kids is the essence of the mission.

32

Keep Pushing for Systemic Change

The longer I teach, the more unrealized potential I see—in students, in myself and my colleagues to reach and inspire them, and especially in the school system that is supposed to support teaching and learning. Corruptions and hubris, politics and laziness, all keep conspiring to undermine our efforts. My priority will always be the needs of the students I have the honor of teaching. For their sake and for the sake of all kids, I am not ever going to shut up about the systemic stupidities and corruption.

You ought never feel reluctant to speak up or speak out about them, either.

Educating children matters, as much as anything—to our nation's economy and well-being, to democracy and public safety—and educating people about what is going on in schools matter. Teachers know better than anyone what is happening in classrooms and schools. Our voices matter.

Everyone's Concern

Most of the people I know outside of work, friends and family, care about the state of our public schools—even those whose children are adults or attend private schools. They should care how their tax dollars are spent and whether we are preparing kids to be productive and engaged citizens.

Strangers often ask me about the state of our schools. They want to hear a public-school teacher's perspective and be disabused of whatever misconceptions they have. The truth about schools and kids is powerful, however narrow or specific our lens. In fact, it is the specificity that is most meaningful, though much of what is wrong with our schools turns out to be quite universal. Some of the people I talk to about these things have already heard from other teachers they know, and usually, what I am telling them is consistent with what they have already heard.

I am always ready to help people understand what is wrong with our schools—the misguided priorities, the lack of imagination, the fear and loathing and in some cases cynicism of people in charge—and I am also always anxious to help people imagine solutions.

> If all of us articulate the realities we experience and observe in our classrooms and schools, we can make an impact.

Raising awareness is an endless endeavor. It is humbling and also hopeful. The few people I talk to tell other people, and ideas filter through segments of the collective consciousness. If all of us articulate the realities we experience and observe in our classrooms and schools, we can make an impact.

Be a Force in the Town Square

For more than a decade, I've been venting my frustration and outrage in op-eds for a variety of publications. I try not to be delusional about the reach and influence of my words in this tiny corner of the media and hope that they are echoed by other educators in other places.

I am happy when a reader reaches out to thank me for articulating something they too have seen or experienced. I am also happy to hear from readers who disagree—those who are civil about it—and have exchanged ideas with strangers on issues such as school safety and guns, the criminalization of students of color, and the educating of undocumented students.

I have also been interviewed about education issues by newspaper reporters and the hosts of radio programs, podcasts, and a few television shows and I am often annoyed—though not really surprised—to see education policy and performance discussed in the media without the views of any actual classroom teachers.

More of us need to get on television and other mass media and be a bigger part of the public discourse. I find it outrageous that so-called education experts rarely include any of the people who actually teach children. There are now many teachers blogging and commenting, in print and video on social media, some of it serious, much of it humorous though with a serious undertone. There are also reformed administrators expressing themselves in this way. All these voices add up, but we still ought to push for more representation in discussions about the present and future of education.

Those of us who are parents should be part of the parent rights movement. Lately, the loudest parent voices are those with narrow political agendas and not a lot of knowledge of what actually goes on in schools and classrooms. They have as much right to speak and advocate as anyone else—but so do we, and we should make sure that we are also heard.

Of course, we are living through a time in which, in some places, the outrages are highly political and culturally oppressive and include the banning of books—often by people who have never read them—and religious inculcation in public schools.

Such circumstances should compel us to want to speak out more, though in such circumstances some teachers may be less free to challenge the authorities at all and I would never presume to tell another educator to risk their job. Amid the culture wars our students need, more than ever, reasonable teachers to help them understand what is happening around them and it may be wise to leave the public outrage to those of us who live in places where we still enjoy academic freedom and free speech rights.

Be a Force Within Your School and District

If you have the good fortune to work in a place with a strong teachers' union, you can often have your concerns expressed through the union leadership. I am a strong advocate for labor unions, for teachers and all other workers, and our union's social and political positions usually align with mine—not surprising since they often solicit our input. Still, I prefer to express my views as an individual, and I encourage other educators to do the same.

I remember the first time I yelled over the phone at a school district official. Our school's copier, which almost never worked, was broken again. This was before we had computers or printers, so the copier was the only way to make multiples of anything. I somehow got hold of the name of the bureaucrat responsible for this sorry state of affairs and let him know that he was an empty suit, a sorry excuse for an educator, a useless loser whose job should be dissolved so that we could all have more money in our budget to buy a working copy machine. I don't know how much of my diatribe he bothered listening to before he hung up. I do not recommend advocating positive change in that manner—though it was somewhat satisfying in the moment.

Since then, I have experienced plenty more moments of outrage but have also discovered that there are actually some good people working in administrative and school district offices, people who want to help teachers help students. Tragically, most seem not to trust teachers enough to solicit our input—or they garnish our input in generalized or half-hearted ways—but I believe it is worth our while, whenever possible, to share our insights, whether anyone asks for them or not.

About ten years ago, back when I was an athletic director, I was at a conference for city high school sports. Some district officials, including the head of athletics, were making a presentation about fundraising. At the time, schools were required to pay for most of the basics of having sports teams—facilities (if they didn't have them on-campus), officials, uniforms, health and safety. For many of us, this was a tremendous burden. Students were made to sell popcorn or discount coupon books or any number of other fundraiser schemes, and most of the revenue came from teachers and families and in impoverished inner-city communities, where students could not safely try to sell to neighbors—they struggled to raise these funds.

Many of us shared the frustration with the district's refusal to fully fund athletics, which the district hierarchy should have understood was an essential motivator for many at-risk students (a gang-prevention program for some) and an important part of every athlete's education with opportunities to learn teamwork, hard work, and sportsmanship—the ability to deal positively with adversity.

In the middle of the fund-raiser rules and regulations PowerPoint, one of the athletic directors rose out of his seat and confronted the head of athletics. "Is athletics a part of instruction?" he asked, to which the director of athletics said, yes, it was. "Doesn't the education code strictly prohibit requiring students and parents to pay for instructional materials and other instructional necessities?" Most of us knew the answer to his question. The district officials all knew. A silence hung in the room as everyone awaited a response. The district officials looked at each other and the head of athletics gave an honest answer.

By the end of that year, the district funded all basic athletic expenses.

I know that AD. We work at the same school now. He is a hero. And I know the head of athletics, who is also a hero for his honesty and humility and the courage to fight his bosses for what was right on behalf of student-athletes. There really are good people in positions of power—and we really can help them do the right thing.

Even the craven and corrupt can be swayed if we understand their fear and avarice. Admins and officials who are ambition-driven can be persuaded if we appeal to that ambition by selling our message as a means by which they can look good and curry favor with their supervisors.

I have seen administrators influenced by their most passionate and effective teachers. I have even seen them set aside fear and ambition and stand up to their bosses on behalf of teachers and students.

So I will always be respectfully outspoken with administrators. In fact, being open and direct with them about my disagreements is the highest expression of respect; it says that I see them as reasonable and open-minded and smart enough to listen to the people doing the most important work of the school.

It helps that I do my job well and that I don't usually do things that make their job any harder than it already is. Sometimes, I might get a little heated in expressing my dismay at a policy or decision, but I never make it personal. Of course, my rants are mostly ignored in the moment but, of course, I am playing the long game. That assistant principal I'm ranting at today might have a more powerful position one day, might even one day be a superintendent or secretary of education—a former colleague of mine now sits on the L.A. School Board!—and maybe something I say will resonate with them somehow, and influence them in some small way.

We have to hope. And never forget our value.

If we are brilliant at what we do, they can never replace us. If we are powerful in our commitment to and connection with kids, they can hardly undermine us, and the more they are compelled to recognize our individualism and talent. Don't hesitate to remind them what good teaching really is. Don't be afraid to let them know how great you are. It is our effectiveness, our unique value, that gives us the right to speak. Don't let anyone, whatever their title or power, tell you otherwise.

It All Starts and Ends in the Classroom

If our collective purpose really is educating our students, enlightening them in the most profound ways, which is to say teaching them about themselves and the world around them and their relationship to it, then shouldn't we be helping them understand the institutions that dominate their lives—political, economic, and educational?

I am not sure that public school administrators or districts appreciate such transparency but to oppose including such truths in a child's education is malpractice and anti-democracy.

I am not advocating the preaching of a political philosophy. Nor the promoting of an agenda, including that of any teacher's union, much as I support their work. What I am proposing is objective and evidence based. The kids in our class will inherit it all—the entire enterprise, good, bad, and really bad. They have a right to know as much about it as possible, and we have a responsibility to tell them the truth.

We may not be entirely neutral. No one ever is. But if we are honest with them and confess our biases, then we greatly reduce the risk that we are brainwashing them to make the world the way we wish it was. Hopefully, instead, we are training them to imagine a better world for themselves and the generations to come.

Some students will remember us after they leave school. They might one day reach out to us or come back and thank us.

If they do, wonderful. But that is trivial.

What really matters is that our work will be embedded in small ways in everything they accomplish. Not our views. Not our biases or our corny jokes or even our words of inspiration. What matters is that we have shown them how to think for themselves and care about people, to have an open mind and heart and to respect science and scholarship and rely on empirical evidence, to question authority and doubt zealots, and to value human life everywhere and see our shared humanity more than our differences, cultural or otherwise.

> What really matters is that our work will be embedded in small ways in everything they accomplish.

If I sound ridiculously idealistic, that is probably because I am. So are all the best teachers I know. It is why we keep pushing to make the system better, advocating for kids while we push them to be better. Idealism—however ridiculous—gives us a reason to get up every morning and muster the energy to coax the successive throngs of addled teenagers into expanding their minds and inspire them to bravely stumble toward the uncertain future.

For Product Safety Concerns and Information please contact our EU representative GPSR@taylorandfrancis.com
Taylor & Francis Verlag GmbH, Kaufingerstraße 24, 80331 München, Germany

www.ingramcontent.com/pod-product-compliance
Lightning Source LLC
Chambersburg PA
CBHW050440240426
43661CB00055B/2454